I FILMED THE HORRORS THE BADDIES THE KILLS and THE DEAD

The Poptastic life of cartoonist and video cameraman

DICKY HOWETT

NEW HAVEN PUBLISHING LTD

Published 2023

NEW HAVEN PUBLISHING LTD
www.newhavenpublishingltd.com
newhavenpublishing@gmail.com

Cover Design © Pete Cunliffe

Introduction

Dicky Howett sold his first cartoon in 1962 to the TV TIMES. He has since produced many thousands of humorous illustrations for publications worldwide. Initially working as a photographic assistant in a London advertising studio, Dicky later joined the BBC at Ealing Studios to train in film handling and editing. A further career move found Dicky working on comics for IPC (Supermum) and Marvel UK (Doctor Who?) Dicky now co-owns one of the world's largest specialist prop houses, GOLDEN AGE TV which rents vintage video and movie equipment for film and television productions. Some are small scale (a microphone) and some larger (an entire tv studio). Currently Dicky and colleagues are working on several projects for Disney, ITV and BBC

"It's only in the immensity of space that one senses cosmic truth"

For Margaret, Lucy, Catherine, Liz, Lily,
Poppy, Toby, Teasel, Nell.
Chaps in this family are definitely outnumbered!

Content

Let's Start At the Very Beginning   7

Off To Work We Go   20

To Ealing With Feeling   25

To The Palace   31

Watch This Space   34

Feeling A Touch Crabby Today   40

Look East Young Man   45

Supermum Does A Spot Of Clubbing   49

Enter The Mighty Marvel Quinn   56

Is It A Dummy Or Is It Noel?   61

Radio And The Write Stuff   67

Two Celebrity Twits On Tv   76

The Higher We Go   83

I Go Clubbing   85

Propping Up   91

Inside The Inside Of Number 9   108

Hollywood Daze   110

Buckets Of Blood And Lots Of Gore   112

I Was Kylie's Cameraman   115

Video Daze   117

Pilot Lights   130

Back To The Grind   133

Tail Pieces   134

All Get Set   144

Hippy No Great Shakes   152

History it Isn't   158

Cartoon Capers   161

Let's Start at the Very Beginning.....

The Horrors The Baddies The Kills and The Dead, what's that all about then? Well, I'm being a little cute here because these are the names of various pop bands, (past and perhaps present),that I've had the exquisite pleasure of filming. But a bit more of this later. Spooling way way back, it was when I was barely 6-weeks old, sitting quietly having a doze with my mother, when suddenly I was embroiled in the ultimate horrors of the baddies the kills and the dead!

It was Adolf Hitler (who was a horror a baddie and a killer all on his own). Let me tell you what that *schweinehund* did to me. It was on the 26th January 1945 at 9.45am bright and early. Our cosy Essex avenue is quiet, then all of a sudden down rushes, at the speed of sound, a V2 rocket which blows the street and our house to smithereens. Right on top of me and my mother. Eight houses demolished, 15 badly damaged and a crater 53'x25'. Three fatalities and 36 serious injuries. Demonstrably we survived. Apparently this was due mainly to my mother hearing, whilst we were buried under a ton of house, an ethereal voice from heaven telling her, *IT WILL BE ALL RIGHT.* Praise be, and so it was, at least so far.

My heart usually sinks when attempting to read autobiographies of alleged celebrities. One is initially introduced to the activities of various great-grandfathers and their Great War experiences. Or great-uncle Gilbert and his extremely boring time fighting the Boars (and bores), and what great-grandma did whilst sipping genteel tea with Mrs Simpson or Attila The Hun or whomever.

I'm not going to begin in that fashion and in any case I'm not an alleged celebrity, just a real one. I *could* say that my maternal great grandfather was a Suffolk master thatcher or my paternal great grandfather was a soup waiter on the Midland Railway. I could add that my maternal grandfather (a Pitmans shorthand champion and freelance private secretary) worked briefly for Winston Churchill. But in this instance I won't mention any of that.

Dicky and Mum in May 1945 looking remarkably unaffected
by their brush with sudden death a few months earlier

So, cutting the infantile years, let's leap in one mighty bound to the beginning of the 1950s and the *Eagle* comic. And this is where the story really begins. The Eagle publication loomed large in my young life with *Dan Dare Pilot of the Future*, featuring prominently in full colour on the front pages. I ignored the rest of the comic. I was not at all interested in cutaway drawings of internal combustion mechanicals, or the lives of various good guys (on the back pages) or *Riding the Range* (even though written by Charles Chilton of *Jet Morgan* fame). However, I did notice that a certain 'Frank Hampson' drew *Dan Dare*. To be frank, I wanted to be Frank. (It was only years later that I discovered that Hampson's studio staff completed most of the finished artwork, copied in minute detail from Frank's immaculate roughs and visuals). I was an avid follower of Dan's adventures, initially with the exquisite story *Operation Saturn* (I joined the comic in 1953 so there it all starts) and I was immediately immersed in the evil doings of the Green Treens and the Mekon and Doctor Blasco (an early exposure here, you will notice, to a fictional Doctor – albeit an evil one) plus Space Fleet rockets piloted by a bunch of RAF-type Johnnies, in smart green uniforms, collars and ties nipping off to Venus at many 'hundreds' of miles an hour and taking approximately a weekend to complete the interplanetary crossing. This, it must be noted, was all performed in the far future of '1996' using little more than a few gallons of upgraded aviation fuel and an electronics box full of thermionic valves. The artwork, of course, was superb.

My admiration for Dan and Co wavered somewhat when in 1955, the *Junior Express Weekly* hit the stands, presenting me with a new space hero, Jeff Hawke 'Pioneer of Space Travel' (The Sydney Jorden strip was a regular feature in the *Daily Express* from 1955 to 1974). The *Junior Express Weekly* was offering readers an exclusive *Jeff Hawke Crew Membership* and the chance to own a special space 'log book'. I applied for mine and was rewarded by being selected as an 'astral navigator'. Not exactly what I wanted, (what was an 'astral' anyway?) The other choices were Radar and Radio, Rocket Engineer and the best, Space Pilot. My pass book was stamped 'passed A1' which was small comfort. However, I did find time to complete a page requiring a 'description of the holder'. I wrote my name, address (in case I got lost in space) age and weight. For a puny eleven year old I gave my weight as 4st and 9 oz. (Perhaps I was thinking of a couple of sacks of spuds at the time?) I still have this log book and, believe it or not, I'm now quite a bit heavier.

Radio was big in the 1950s and none bigger than an epic twenty-week rocket ship saga that attracted twenty million listeners, and me. 'The BBC presents Jet Morgan in *Journey into Space...*!' so intoned the sepulchral voice of David Jacobs at the beginning of one of BBC Radio's most successful series of the 1950s. Conceived written and produced by Charles Chilton, these seminal stories of space-flight and strange goings on in space captured the public imagination. Every Monday evening at 7.30 pm, the latest cliff-(or in this case asteroid-)hanger was resolved, only to later plunge the listening millions into yet another week of anxious nail chewing anticipation. This vastly popular series (David Lean even proposed doing a movie version) emptied pubs and caused factory workers to forsake overtime. The programme was considered a landmark in popular radio drama. From 1953 through to 1955, the BBC made a trilogy of programmes consecutively entitled, *Journey into Space* (re-recorded in 1958 as *Operation Luna*), *The Red Planet* and *The World in Peril*. Each episode was recorded on tape and the evocative background music, composed and conducted by Van Phillips, was swung off discs in situ. Sound effects likewise, these having been recorded at Battersea Power Station and the National Physical Laboratory at Kingston. (The ominous 'tele-viewer' sound was, in fact, naval ASDIC). But it was all myth and magic to me. Jet Morgan and crew landing on the Moon and then being whisked back in time to a prehistoric Earth. Were the pictures better on radio? Immeasurably.

Although a working class and relatively threadbare family we, in our house, had a television set. It was a little nine inch black and white Ecko table model and *The Quatermass Experiment* was on! This was a monumental six-part creeping horror of a serial, broadcast live, direct from the BBC's cramped and very outdated studios situated at Alexandra Palace. So the story goes, a spaceship crash lands and 'something' emerges from the wreckage. It looks like a man, but is it...? Basic stuff, but back then we had not seen the like, and the TV nation sat transfixed. I recall now only one scene, this from episode five. The camera tracked back to reveal a park bench with a couple sitting on it, chatting away. As the couple leave, the camera pans down and we see 'something' rustling in the bushes behind them. Wooo-hooo. I watched nearly all the episodes but missed the final part due to my mother failing to wake me in time (I had to pretend to go to bed as my younger brother wasn't allowed to watch 'horror films'). There was no chance of seeing again the bulk of this TV production as only the first two parts were preserved as recordings. But back then telly was supposed to be live and in any case, tele-recording (a linked 35mm film camera looking at a monitor screen) was expensive. Generally, the unions and the cinema industry were quite sniffy about any form of television 'copying', especially drama.

In June 1953 the very biggest live telly event of that decade was the coronation broadcast of our late Queen Elizabeth. For this, the BBC deployed all of its latest camera equipment with the crews required to wear lounge suits and ties. In one instance, a cameraman was bedecked in full evening dress. During the run up to the coronation date, the nation frantically acquired television sets, and those that didn't, insinuated themselves towards neighbours who had. When June 6th arrived did we invite all our neighbours and friends in to watch the proceedings on our little Ecko? Not a bit of it. Inexplicably, me and my family totally avoided the 'great day' and went on a trip to Southend-on-Sea. We got wet.

Hardly anyone now admits to watching early BBC television and only three people and a parrot recall the actual opening, in November 1936 (using a Baird 240 line non-interlaced mechanical film/spotlight system), of the BBC's very own 'world's first high-definition' television service. (This is of course, not to be confused with the various Russian/American/French/Italian/Dutch/German television services that were already planned). These days, the early history of television comes across as a myth, with claims and counter-claims specifically devised to confuse the unwary, and in particular, latter-day tv-programme researchers who manifestly get it wrong. (Children recently interviewed thought tv started as long ago as 1970! If only..)

A friend of mine, Don Weston watched in wonder the stumbling efforts of pre-war BBC 405-line tv. He said that sometimes the 'bullseye' (picture shading where the middle was dark and the edges light) got very bad. Occasionally, live transmission was halted because of the dire image quality. Also, cathode ray tube ion burn was a particular problem. I suppose the minuscule audience at the time endured it stoically, sitting patiently, (as doubtless they were), in full evening kit with copious quantities of Gin & It on tap and the butler at standby.

My father said he remembers watching in 1937, an outside broadcast from a theatre where throughout the entire performance the *single* live camera was locked-off at dress circle height. This, presumably was an experiment, an attempt to reproduce a 'seat' in the auditorium. Riveting stuff.

Of course, back in those grey valve-driven days, the technology was the *thing;* the latest gadget. Television aerials were real (and enormous) status symbols. Proto-tv was in black and white because it just *was.* It didn't seem at all strange that each evening we squinted up-close at a 10x8" inch image. Also, those old-style tv screens were edged with a curious cream-coloured thick plastic collar which seemed to serve no useful purpose except collect nicotine stains easily, (at least it did in our house). The entire ensemble was usually mounted in a naff imitation oak wooden box with the addition a cheap reading lamp plonked on top (well we don't want to strain our eyes do we, dear?).Ah, but at least the *lines* were sharp and the whistle was sometimes louder than Granny's hearing aid and the picture screamed when things got too contrasty. Once, our television set actually blew up precisely at the point when the *Saturday Night Out* title sequence road sign burst in star fashion (at the sound of a cymbal) to disclose the upcoming programme. We peered expectantly at the smoking screen, thinking it was all part of the show.

But I hadn't neglected my Destiny. Much time was spent after school in the privacy of my own bedroom, drawing *Superman* strips, little quarter-page four-frame efforts with my own glowing text strap-lines on the title page, '*He could out-race a speeding rocket*' – picture of Supie speeding past a rocket. '*His strength knows no limit*' – Supie lifts a block of flats, and '*He can squeeze water from a stone*'. A bit unlikely perhaps, but I recall that in one of the movies, Superman squeezed a fully-cut diamond from a mere lump of coal so I suppose anything is possible.

Actually Supie is flying the wrong way!. Strips go usually left to right, the way we scan a page of text etc. Well I never did., and in this case, I didn't.

Another definite 1950s cartoon favourite of mine was *Garth*. A *Daily Mirror* newspaper strip, Garth was an all-British mighty man with mythical overtones. Jumping ahead a bit to 1965, I had the pleasure of meeting *Garth*'s creator Steve Dowling and assistant John Allard, (and later, pre-eminent *Garth* script writer Peter O'Donnell). This was for an article I was considering writing for my amateur science fiction fanzine *Spot Wobble*. And so it was with unbelievable ease that I sauntered into the *Mirror* offices (long-since demolished) in High Holborn. During our chat, puffing on his pipe, Steve Dowling sketched before my very eyes, a panel for the following week's *Garth* adventure. Effortless skill. When Steve retired, the strip was taken over and drawn by, among others, Frank Bellamy. Not, I fear Frank's finest achievement. His signature 'cinematic' style of artwork gradually coarsened the tone of the strip. Also, Frank had difficulty drawing the nude female form convincingly – '*blokes with tits*' was one pointed comment – and the strip lost much subtlety in the process. A case of 'dumbing down' before the epithet became synonymous. In my eyes *Garth* never really recovered when its originators departed.

Steve Dowling drawing GARTH

14

A year or two ago I was contacted by a video producer working on a *Garth* documentary. He asked me about the possibility of using the photographs I had taken during my Dowling interview. It now appears that these pictures (just three) are the only existing record of Steve Dowling at work on the *Garth* strip. A piece of cartoon history fortuitously preserved. Chuffed or what?

Although my youthful cartooning attempts kept me off the streets, television encroached again. This occurred one bank holiday during a visit to Southend-on-Sea. Strolling along the prom, I encountered an actual outside broadcast taking place. Television in the 1950s was all-live, and being all-live it needed regular injections of action and adventure. Outside broadcasting provided some ready-made thrills and, in those years, a favourite thrilling venue for both BBC and ITV was Southend-on-Sea. Never a year seemed to go by without Southend Pier (longest in the world at 1¼ miles) or its famous Carnival being featured on Saturday afternoon telly, sandwiched between the regular diet of all-in wrestling, show jumping and boat racing.

On the basis that any old excuse would do (from a bank holiday to a coronation), the TV companies would rush instantly, van loads of cameras and miles of cable to any likely festive vantage point, but not *too* far from London. Nationwide television was still a few years away and in the mid-1950s, ITV was several Companies short of a network. The actual subject seemed not to matter. Everything was new and it was all grist to the TV mill. Indeed, for years, a Southend seafront gypsy fortune-teller had a sign displayed which read proudly: 'As featured on BBC Television'. Doubtless the seekers of fortune were suitably impressed.

But it was Southend Carnival that provided the ultimate black and white TV attraction. In 1956, the commercial tv company ATV transmitted the festivities, setting up their cameras and control vans beside the old swimming pool at nearby Westcliff. Included in the day's programme was a beauty contest (typical ITV) from the pool. Later in the afternoon, a proportion of the carnival procession was televised. For this, two cameras were used, one mounted on a dolly beside the road and the other, high on a gantry using a new-fangled zoom lens. What all these Southend programmes actually looked like, I now have only fragmentary recollections. Old TV-Timers will tell you that these O.B.s were fraught with technical and artistic problems. Cameras would focus on the wrong item or break down at critical moments. Commentators would lose their sound-leads or drop their microphones. Interviewees would freeze-up in panic and forget their own names. Strange and inexplicable pauses proliferated. Everything over-ran. And it always seemed to be raining.

Southend 1956. Dreaming of tv cameras.
I now own about 30......

Television outside broadcasting was not new. It began as far back as the early 1930s. On May 8th 1931, Scottish innovator, John Logie Baird loaded a mechanical 30-line picture scanner into a wood-clad holiday caravan, trundled this into the street outside his London Long Acre workshop and relayed (if only across a few yards) an image from 'outside'. Later, that same year on June 3rd, Baird took his TV caravan down to Epsom and broadcast live scenes from the Derby (the first sports O.B.) via the BBC medium wave transmitter at Brookman's Park. A bold technological feat considering the totally uncharted TV territory and the haphazard nature of the telephone lines that linked the system. The pictures of the Derby (actually just the winning post area) were barely recognizable (viewers thought the horses looked like blurred camels). The poor image quality was due to electrical interference and the low bandwidth used. But a precedent had been established. O.B.s worked! Although Baird's creaky TV system was abandoned ultimately as impractical, the publicity value of such demonstrations spurred further developments, especially in all-electronic television.

Elsewhere in Europe, at the 1936 Berlin Olympic Games, the German experimental TV service used two O.B. vans feeding a mixture of 180-line electronic and semi-live intermediate-film pictures (film shot first then quickly developed – very quickly, about 45 seconds – and then passed through a scanner beam). But the first *all-electronic* high definition 405-line outside broadcast unit was built in 1937 for BBC Television. The unit comprised two Regal vans built by AEC of Southall and equipped by the Marconi-EMI company. A third vehicle carried the 1kw VHF link transmitter. The unit supplied all the necessary control apparatus. This included two vision monitors and four microphone inputs. Three 'Emitron' cameras supplied the pictures and on May 12th 1937 the unit televised live the coronation procession of King George VI. With these outside broadcasts, early television established an audience, (about 10,000 watched the transmission) and importantly, it helped to sell sets.

Unfortunately, no official recordings exist of any of those pre-war broadcasts. There does reside somewhere in the BBC archives a brief snatch of blurry amateur footage showing the 1937 coronation live pictures filmed off the screen. This was taken by a Marconi employee using his own 16mm camera running at a very slow speed in order to get an exposure. The pictures on pre-war tv sets were quite dim.

None of the 1950s Southend Carnival outside broadcasts were

recorded either. They were not exactly historic, nor considered at the time worthy of any sort of archive preservation. My memories of that 1956 Southend Carnival are reinforced by the photographs my father and I took of the television technical gear. But I shall always recall, fondly, the remark made to me by an ATV cameraman who was filming the carnival. As a TV camera-mad twelve year old, I confessed to him that I wanted to be a TV cameraman when I grew up. 'Bugger off, can't you see I'm working?' he muttered helpfully. But I wasn't abashed by these pearls of advice. It was but a mere forty years later that I actually achieved my ambition.

And so it transpired that during the entire 1950s, a spotty telly-potty kid was I, inflicted with a strange yearn for a taste of TV technology: the camera, the lights, the studio, the lot. I applied regularly for free audience tickets to BBC television variety productions (ITV studios had a higher audience age limit of sixteen years, thus I was then too young to enter, so BBC shows it had to be). They included long forgotten productions such as *The Ted Ray Show* and *The Billy Cotton Band Show*, highlights of Saturday night typical BBC telly, all produced live and dripping from an old converted West London theatre, the Shepherd's Bush Empire, on Shepherd's Bush Green. A visit to the Empire (renamed in 1953, the BBC Television Theatre) was always an adventure, a trip to the Big Bad City and a chance to see real TV cameras in action! For an impressionable nipper, it was an exciting time, full of mystery and wonder.

Those early tv shows, however, appeared far *better* in the flesh than they appeared on the home screen. At the time, BBC light entertainment (as opposed presumably, to BBC *heavy* entertainment) ran a very poor second -with less than 30% of the audience- to the glamorous and flashy ITV. However, most noticeable and most startling to anyone new to the sight of a television studio was the sheer colour of it all. Also the clear, vibrant quality of the live audio. Unfortunately, in the nineteen fifties both those technical factors were missing from the average cheapo 405-line domestic monochrome telly.

In fact, strange to relate, those old-time tv stars were not instantly recognisable in the flesh, so used as we were to viewing them in 'glorious' black and white. My mum (who accompanied me to several shows) was utterly convinced that a handsome BBC stage-hand was the pianist Russ Conway. Whereas all the while, the real Russ Conway, (known for his twinkling smile and full front set) was sitting dumpy, hunched and unglamorous at the side of the stage awaiting his cue. When Russ come on to play a tune, my Mum actually thought <u>he</u> was an impostor, because he didn't 'look' anything like his appearance on the home screen! Such was the power of television in those days. Performers were regarded reverentially, as some sort of super-beings from outer space, and not like real people at all. Things haven't changed much.

One of my 1950s tv cameras. Compare with page 17
Haven't changed much have I......?

Off to Work We Go

Time to leave school, and with absolutely no academic qualifications whatsoever, what to do? In 1959- and this is true- there were jobs aplenty. A friend at the time changed jobs every week! So here was me with nothing to offer but a clutch of artless *Superman* cartoons, but I was very keen to learn. With very little effort, I gained employment in London as an office boy being paid £4 a week, working at an advertising art studio called Pentagon Design Services. This outfit had premises in Rupert Street, Soho, W1. Pentagon Design Services consisted of three febrile and cramped floors of closet pederasts, neo-Nazis and dipsy Scotsmen. Naturally, I was oblivious to the implications of all this. I was, after all, only fifteen years old and had never before met a real Scotsman.

Rupert Street was on the edge of London's Theatre Land and the place abounded with 'colourful' characters, including a coffee bar paedophile who used to regularly try and tempt me (unsuccessfully) by producing something out of his trouser pocket, but it was only a chunk of amber with a fly trapped in it. Some mornings, when I arrived for work, the street would be littered with drunks and sad to say, our little design studio regularly had its early morning doorstep milk delivery nicked by opportunistic and thirsty derelicts. Further into the working day, groups of strolling tinker street musicians would wander down Rupert Street. These melodious minstrels received our undivided attention. A favourite trick was to hurl pennies down to their out-stretched hands ('tank you soor...') but first we fully-heated the coins to cherry red over our kettle gas ring. Another juvenile jape was to squirt lighter fluid under the lavatory door (when occupied by unsuspecting colleagues) then light and retire. At other idle moments we played darts. Our skills were variable, culminating once in a well-placed missile imbedding itself, double top, into somebody's thigh.

My daily working routine consisted of ferrying around London, artwork produced by the studio (nothing very elaborate, just small illustrations for patent pharmaceuticals or kitchen cutlery) to various clients. Occasionally, 1 took artwork to the commercial television companies. All this was very exciting. At the time, they had premises in Hanover Square (ABC TV), Golden Square (Granada TV) and Great Cumberland Place (ATV) Sometimes 1 delivered material to an imposing ITV building in Kingsway (once called Adastral House, formally home to the Air Ministry) and now aptly rechristened Television House. This was the home of Associated- Rediffusion Ltd (it also contained the studios of ITN plus an office for Scottish Television). Very glam – lots of potted plants, sleek decor and even sleeker lady receptionists! Heaven. The advertising artwork that 1 diligently transported consisted of short messages, (perhaps illustrated), constructed as 10x12 inch captions used in 'spot' commercials. It was simple, direct stuff. No fancy video shoots or clever angles. Just a bit of cardboard, but cardboard or not, it certainly made money for everyone, especially the television companies. For example, back in 1961 one could purchase from ATV (in the Midlands) a five second slide, with announcer's voice-over, on the afternoon show *Lunch Box* for fifteen quid. At peak times the cost of an ATV five second slot rocketed to a staggering £70! By way of financial contrast, the *all- day* five second price on Ulster Television was a mere £8. ABC TV by comparison would charge for five seconds a weekend top rate (Sunday evenings) of £576. But that was the cheaper end of the television advertising market. The expensive stuff (at 1961 prices in the London or Midlands area) ran at an average £1,000 for an ordinary 30-second peak-time airing of a professionally filmed commercial which had probably cost at least £5,000 to make. Riveting information as you doubtless can appreciate.

Quite soon, I was promoted, from office boy to negative-sorter. The top floor of Pentagon Design Services had a small photographic department run by a rabid anti-Semite (he claimed – amongst other racist things – that Jewish tailors were no big deal and so he set about, and indeed succeeded, in making his own bespoke sports coat). Eric, for that was his name, also had a phobia about being photographed. Ironic for a photographer, one would have thought? But Eric died soon after of lung cancer (not as a direct result of his bigotry I hasten to add) and so I moved up a notch. I was again promoted, this time to the running of the D&P (Develop and Print) section. I got so proficient I could actually develop and print without the need of timers or measures. It became almost second nature (A skill curiously now no longer required since the advent of digital photography).

Lunch hours (plus sandwiches) were spent in various West End News Theatres, a now long-abandoned form of cinema that showed the latest newsreels from Pathe, Gaumont British, or Movietone News. Padding the News was a string of elderly comedy 'shorts' from beyond the Hollywood grave. *The Three Stooges* or *Laurel and Hardy*, plus cartoons from Disney. Also MGM's *Tom and Jerry* or Warner's, *Tweety Pie and Sylvester* (the best). I sat through my very favourite, a Chuck Jones classic called *One Froggy Evening* about twenty times, soggy sandwiches forgotten.

Thus cartoons were never far away. I was still scribbling in my spare time and I must confess that to this day, I'm not certain who suggested I try and actually *sell* my cartoons. In our house newspapers were the *Daily Mirror*, and the *Daily Sketch* with the weekly *TV Times*, all of which had glorious cartoon pages displaying the works of cartoonists with curious signatures like 'Clew', 'Chic', 'Waller', 'Whimsy' or 'Styx'. So I gave it a try and submitted a few 'single' cartoons. My cartoon jokes were pretty standard for the time, mothers-in-law, stupid wives, stupid policemen, stupid kids, that sort of non-PC thing and my cartoon style of drawing was very awkward and undistinguished. Nothing sold for a few months, and then, Bang! A sale! My very first and it was to the *TV Times*. My cartoon was printed in their 'Natural Break' cartoon page. I was paid the fabulous sum of three guineas.(£3.3 shillings) It was 1962 and I seemed to be well and truly on my way.

However, as a photographer, I was still learning my trade. I would often take my lovely Yashica Mat twin lens reflex camera (poor man's Rollieflex) out and about, loaded with a roll of Ilford HP3 120 film. I still have, filed away, some nice shots in and around Liverpool Street Station, Piccadilly Circus and the River Thames at night, all historic views now. I also took several Soho scenes featuring the occasional celebrity wandering the streets. David Frost was one such, plus a hasty snap of a curious looking exhibitionist being hauled along in a cart. The exhibitionist I later identified as a (then) nonentity called Jimmy Savile. He was being trundled around London for a St Albans Student Rag Week. Little did we know... but at the time I was just snapping away with no thought of future times and events. I printed all my own work and the processing was free. However, the job at Pentagon was beginning to pawl. I was reaching that stage when something new seemed to beckon, and that 'something new' was BBC2.

Watch out, there's a paedo about! Savile and helpers in 1962 Charing Cross Road all unawares.

Piccadilly Circus circa 1962

To Ealing With Feeling

The BBC had been granted a second television channel which opened on April 20th 1964, so popular on the night it blew all the lights in West London (or so it would have seemed). They were fast recruiting staff and I answered an advertisement in a trade journal seeking anyone interested. I do mean *anyone*. In past times, the old civil service-style BBC had insisted on a few qualifications, basic school certificates etc. I had none. However, never tardy about hiding my bushel under a light, I applied for a post as a 'film assistant', citing my previous professional negative-sorting plus nascent photographic work and also my precocious ventures into amateur 16mm filming. I explained that I had shot a few scenes at the 1961 Radio Show at Earls Court when the BBC had first shown colour TV to the public at large (this footage can now be seen in its entirety somewhere on YouTube). I neglected to mention in my application that I would have gaily sawn off my right leg to become a BBC Television employee!

So it came to pass that I started my first BBC job (with all limbs attached) on March 16th 1964 for the grand yearly sum of £690. I had to get a bank account and even wear a tie. I was employed as a 'Trainee Film Assistant' and I travelled each day from Harold Wood in Essex to Ealing Film Studios, a daily round trip door-to-door of approximately four hours. But did I care? Hey, I was working at the BBC! Not exactly BBC *Television*, indeed I never, during my brief BBC career, worked at the tv studios at Lime Grove, Riverside or Television Centre. I was based at Ealing, or as the BBC entitled it 'TFS' (Television Film Studios). But at least it had the word *Television* in the title and I did get to meet a Dalek.

In 1955, the BBC bought the famous Ealing Film Studios and in 1956 transferred all their film 'effort' as they liked to term it. At the time, BBC Television used a vast quantity of film (actually more than Hollywood) which included film inserts to live programming like *Z Cars* or *Tonight*. Also nature footage for wildlife productions with David Attenborough or special documentaries (Elgar, Debussy) for *Monitor*, directed by luminaries such as Ken Russell. During my time at Ealing the biggest production progressing was a vast landmark 26-episode BBC2 series called *The Great War*. Sardonic comments by staff indicated that this production was taking more resources to produce and finish than the Great War itself.

Ealing boasted three large production studios, thirty two cutting rooms, lighting and camera departments, a film vault, a dubbing theatre and a film review suite, which is where I worked. Me and my colleagues ran projectors and sound reproducers, showing various bits of film footage including rushes, complete programmes or library appraisals. BBC film cameraman Nat Crosby reckoned we were all 'young enthusiasts' waiting for an opportunity to graduate to the camera department. Maybe, but for the time being it was nice just standing around being paid to watch movies all day long. Initially our Bell & Howell 609 projectors used carbon arc lamps, (which needed trimming and watching to make certain the 'arc' gap didn't get too wide) but soon changed to Xenon lamps for an easier working life. Also by the mid-1960s, 16mm film was supplanting the use of 35mm in television production and so gradually, all our 35mm projectors (bar two) were replaced.

The 'Dalek' episode was somewhat unremarkable, inasmuch as an inert wood and tin TV prop frightens absolutely nobody, with the exception of a small child (on a staff family visit) who steadfastly refused to venture any further past the props shed where the aforementioned Skaroan was temporarily and visibly housed. It transpired that the Dalek was on day-release from Television Centre. It was going to be filmed for an insert into a BBC2 *Out of the Unknown* drama entitled *Get Off Of My Cloud*, an episode now sadly missing from the BBC archives.

The 'BBC Club' was a great BBC institution, a watering hole for the Corporation-stressed and their guests. To be sure, very little *water* was necessarily consumed, but a visit to 'the Club', (apart from attempting to impress young ladies), was an opportunity to visit BBC television studios and in particular the fabulous Television Centre at White City.

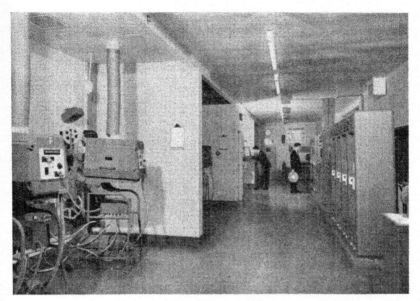

Fig. 17 — Six review theatre suite—general view of section of projection room

Fig. 18 — Six review theatre suite—16-mm projection bay

The projection area at Ealing where I worked. Happy times watching movies all the day long

27

The late-lamented Centre (foolishly sold in 2013 for a mere pittance by the BBC's Head of Bad Moves & National Disgraces) was designed by a true genius architect, Graham Dawbarn who thoughtfully included in the ring doughnut-shaped building, special studio viewing galleries to all the main production areas. Thus, on my various TVC visits I would nonchalantly wander around, peer down excitedly and observe rehearsals and recordings.

Doctor Who and the Sensorites was one such. This was being recorded in Studio 3 with William Hartnell and Carole Ann Ford, whom I distinctly recall 'dancing' about as the end music played and the captions rolled. I apprised Carole of this memory when I met her in 2013 during my filming on the set of the BBC commemorative *Doctor Who* drama, *An Adventure in Space and Time*. Naturally, Carole had no recollection of her impromptu jig, but was thrilled that I had remembered something so trivial.

One of the perks of BBC employment was priority access to tickets for light entertainment or other programmes requiring an audience. Applications for popular shows were usually oversubscribed, but BBC staff got advance warning of what was coming and so we could all jump the 'queue'. As a result of gaining one of these tickets, I actually appeared for the very first time on television. The programme was a cheap and cheerful production called *Juke Box Jury*.

Juke Box Jury wasn't the most original BBC television programme of the 1960s, but it was certainly one of the most popular and it had a secret ingredient in the shape of, The General Public. *Juke Box Jury*, chaired by genial David Jacobs, first aired in 1959. Initially, it occupied an early evening weekday slot but later, the show was shifted to Saturday peak time in order to compete with ITV's frantic (and innovative) pop show *Boy Meets Girl*. Like most British popular TV programmes of the time, *Juke Box Jury* was adapted from an American original format.

During 1953 in Hollywood, station KNXT (a CBS affiliate) first transmitted the programme, devised and hosted by an engaging character called Peter Potter. The KNXT show, sponsored each week by a variety of products, concentrated on the (usually six) star guests and even had a live music spot. The *raison d'être* of the show was that the celebrity panel displayed their ignorance, wit or

28

judgement about various newly-released popular recorded ditties. Also, the US version had a glamorous 'hostess', who during the playing of the discs, wandered amongst the jurists dispensing 'refreshments'.

The BBC's version of *Juke Box Jury* had fewer jurists (four), and no glamour girl dishing out BBC plonk. The main departure from the US format was that during the disc play, the cameras concentrated on the studio audience, therein laid the success and popular appeal of the programme. People clamoured for tickets just for a chance to be 'on the telly', albeit only for five seconds a shot.

Juke Box Jury was staged at several of the BBC's studio sites, including the Television Theatre at Shepherd's Bush, Lime Grove Studio G and Television Centre Studio 2. It is true that elderly BBC studio commissionaires always had to stand well clear when the audience was admitted because usually there was an almighty stampede for the front row. This was somewhat pointless as the cameras always found faces to shoot wherever they were seated. No amount of admonishing, 'Don't rush, don't rush!' made the slightest difference.

Juke Box Jury was broadcast ostensibly 'live' each Saturday, but what actually occurred was that after the live show was aired, another was recorded. To facilitate this, the audience was judiciously shuffled, the panel changed, the Juke Box re-stuffed and off we went again. This meant of course, that when a lucky member of the audience got 'caught' on camera during the *recorded* show they could catch up with their star performance the following week. This is exactly what happened to me. The following week I had my camera trained on the TV screen and managed to capture a frame of my less than convincing performance as 'a member of the audience'. On one J B J occasion at the Television Theatre, (I was in the studio again) at the end of the live broadcast, the cameras were kept trained on the audience. As the cameras panned about focusing on individuals, this caused a *frisson* around the theatre. It transpired subsequently that a policeman visiting the studio had seen on the monitors a 'wanted' face amongst the audience, though this later turned out not to be the case. Indeed it now appears that the police missed a trick searching for potential criminals because one of the 'Jurors' that day was the odious 'nonentity' Jimmy Savile.

29

Juke Box Jury (even the signature tune was a hit) ended its original BBC run in 1967. The programme resurfaced in 1979 with Noel Edmonds and again in 1989 with Jools Holland honking the hooter, but the original excitement had vanished. It was impossible to recapture those special magic TV moments such as when all four Beatles and later the Rolling Stones were 'jurists'. (all recordings, of course, usefully missing from the BBC archives). And then there was the time when singer Johnny Mathis stuck a clothes peg on his nose in a witty attempt to characterize the 'quality' of a Cliff Richard song. Soon after, Mathis' career in this country went into a bit of a decline.

Me in the audience on Juke Box Jury

To the Palace

Journeying westwards to Ealing every week was beginning to irk. Also, I was at an age when I decided it might be quite nice to live away from home. My current weekly wage was around £15 per week so I could easily afford a bedsit room somewhere nearby. Indeed, what actually happened was that I shifted BBC locations entirely and re-established myself in North London, high atop a hill near Alexandra Palace.

Alexandra Palace (or 'AP' in BBC parlance) was currently the home of Television News. The two original pre-war BBC production studios had closed in 1954, only to be re-inhabited by the fledgling BBC television news organization. Initially, BBC TV News had run a very poor second to the dynamic ITN, but by the mid-1960s (when I turned up, but not because of) things had improved. Richard Baker, Robert Dougall, Michael Aspel and Peter Woods were the 'newsreaders' and very much the stars of the show. I on the other hand was still running projectors, stuck, single-handed in shanty booths, spooling 16mm news footage in very short chunks for the assembled film editors to assess. I can't say that this was the most interesting aspect of my BBC career. Fortunately, several other BBC employees were members of the Finchley Amateur Cine Society, and as I now owned a superior Bolex H16 16mm cine camera I became involved in shooting some of the Society's homemade movie projects.

One dramatic presentation was called *Ivorypaws* and for this epic I shot some footage flying in a light aircraft (looking down on the 'baddies' running around in a field). I also drew and filmed, frame-by-frame, an animated title sequence which was my first and last venture into *Looney Tunes* territory. Not content with a backstage role, I also 'acted' in another amateur offering (*Ratman and Bobbin* – guess what *that* was all about). For this I had to pretend to be a pop singer miming away on a stage with my 'group' behind me. I roped in a friend, Christopher Priest to appear in the 'band'. Christopher Priest is now an award-winning and highly respected author of amongst other titles, 'The 'Prestige' and 'The Dream Archipelago' SF series of books, so it didn't do him any harm. All this merry 16mm filming didn't come cheap. Fortunately, BBC TV News had its own on-site film developing and processing plant, and so naturally, us Finchley Filmsters took advantage of this facility, quite a few times if I recall.

Recently on a tv channel called *Talking Pictures* I saw myself at Alexandra Palace back in 1967 operating a BBC projector. This was part of a short film I had apparently shot at Alexandra Palace for a BBC News film editor chum Wilf Watters. It was entitled 'My Job' and it showed Wilf editing news film. The end credits had me as cameraman. I must have inhabited an alternative universe in those days because I have absolutely no memory of filming this epic. Thanks Wilf for jogging and indeed fogging my brain.

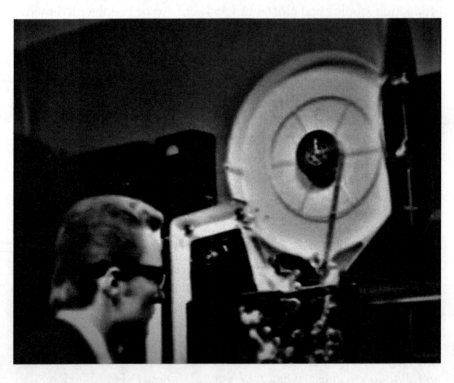

A frame grab from 'My Job' An unremembered 16mm epic

But I was still submitting cartoons to all and sundry, and doing quite nicely too. I was getting published regularly in *The Sun, The Daily Sketch, Titbits, Reveille, News of the World.* However, my

BBC bosses weren't too pleased because 'established' BBC staffers were not supposed to have second 'jobs' (but I knew for a fact that at least one film editor owned a travel agency and another made quite rude films). Eventually, I tried to perk up my working life by changing BBC jobs. I applied for a post as a trainee news film editor, which I attained, but soon lost interest in the truly tedious process of cutting bits of film to a length 15 seconds (or less). And so with some regret, in November 1968 I resigned from the BBC and cashed in my entire BBC pension contributions (£234.18.11d). On that note I left the Corporation for good.

Oh, did I mention a few lines back, 'rude films'. It goes with out saying, (but perhaps it should), that it was not unknown for my steamy projection booth to whirr away occasionally to an engrossed audience, the flickering screen displaying some positively untransmittable images.

Next up: nothing much. Getting married and continuing the path towards my 'Destiny' as a freelance cartoonist. So what could *possibly* go wrong?

Watch This Space

It was 1969 and I was full of optimism. I had married lovely Margaret, whose parents were Buckinghamshire middle class tax collector Tories. And me, a council house boy from Ravensbourne Crescent (sometimes called Rogues Crescent) so they weren't best-pleased to have in the family an out-of-work, sarcastic, artistic scruff. However, blithely ignoring all that, we set up home in a first floor rented flat at 19a Birdhurst Road, South Croydon. Handy for the railway station too, which was nearby with London only twenty minutes door to door.

First car. First and last wife Margaret

I was on my way (or so I thought). First call, *The Daily Mirror*. I had been selling single cartoons to the paper for a few years. Not bad money but not regular. What I needed was a coveted daily contract (or even weekly) to produce a strip cartoon. I roughed out some thoughts and developed an idea (not very original, as it turned out) which, I reasoned, was right up their Fleet Street. *Space Flot* was the title, a 'funny' science research lab with a mad professor, a dippy scientist, an odd-job man and a lab dog who uttered nothing but 'Yip'.

'Nope' was the *Mirror*'s reaction. I tried again with another idea, one about a talking blob of shaving cream called, with faultless logic, 'Blob'. But the main nationals (I even tried to interest *The Times*) were having none of it, or me. To have landed a daily cartoon strip would have earned me quite a bit of kudos and cash. To put that into context, pre-eminent cartoonist Bill Tidy began in 1971 a *Daily Mirror* strip entitled *The Fosdyke Saga*. Bill was interviewed on the BBC's *World At One* by William Hardcastle, who intimated that Bill could now afford to own an Aston Martin DB4! Such dreams.

I continued to sell 'singles', or what was termed 'spot' cartoons. Some publications paid nine guineas, some two quid. But the market then was quite large so there were ample opportunities to make sales. For example, the national red tops had a daily cartoon page, with the *Daily Sketch* having the best. Weekly magazines had them too including *Titbits*, *Reveille*, *Weekend*, *TV Times*, and D.C. Thomson's *Weekly News* (one of the worst rates of pay by the way). My total earnings for 1969 were £807 or about fifteen quid a week. But let us leave the heady world of cartoons for a moment and zoom off into Outer Space.

During the 1960s I discovered the delights of science fiction (or SF as correctly termed, *never* the pejorative 'Sci-Fi'). There existed at the time (and still perhaps does) an organization called The British Science Fiction Association. This Association was fan-based, but with a notable coterie of professional writers. SF fans would socialize at regular intervals and, once a year, would attend (usually at Easter) Conventions dotted around the UK. It was a fun time of lectures by authors, book sales, art shows, fancy dress and booze. Mainly booze. Several BSFA members produced amateur magazines called fanzines, (a creative way of communicating before the era of blogs, Facebook and other internet blessings). Most of these fanzine publications (produced using wax stencils and churned out on Gestetner rotary printers), were execrable, but a few had genuine merit, indeed, several future SF authors contributed as young fans, learning their craft. I had a go too, drawing cartoons and illustrations directly onto these wax stencils, which required a good degree of pre-planning and a steady hand. The results were quite satisfying. I produced my first science fiction 'fanzine' in 1964, and contributed most of the written and drawn contents, none now worth repeating here.

I had also vague dreams of becoming a writer of science fiction stories. I went as far as taking a postal writing course which actually pooh-poohed science fiction as a genre. The instructors were adamant that I should first become proficient at 'proper' writing before attempting anything stupid. I buckled down and actually learnt a few things, such as getting a 'hook' in early to interest the reader. My main difficulty was that I couldn't think of any interesting stories to tell or work out a proper plot. I did actually manage to sell one short story entitled *The Haul*, to *Titbits* magazine. It was co-written with chum Chris Priest (a proper writer). The story was a slice of whimsy concerning an unlucky burglar called Gerry who was foiled stealing a thousand quid life savings from under a bed because it was all in threepenny pieces!

At the time, my favourite SF authors were Bob Shaw, Robert Heinlein, Arthur C. Clarke, Brian Aldiss, Harry Harrison. Phillip K. Dick and Robert Sheckley (and sixty years later they are still). For a relative youngster, science fiction clubdom was good fun and, as intimated, several SF fans went on to greater things; The late Terry Pratchett, Christopher Priest, Mike Ashley, Malcolm Edwards *et al* achieved deserved success as writers, editors or journalists within the genre.

During the mid-1960s there was a flurry of British flying saucer reports. Newspapers published accounts of weird bangs and other loud noises with sightings of strange nocturnal lights in the sky. Photos soon appeared, one depicted an object looking like a flying eye and another of a large alien dish-shaped object resting in a field with a policeman looking at it. As an avid reader of science fiction, this spiked my interest and I began to delve into the subject. A group of local flying saucer enthusiasts had their base in Wood Green near to Muswell Hill where I had my bedsit. I was invited to attend what they termed a 'Sky Watch'. A nearby open space called Crews Hill was chosen to be thus watched from, and so we all trouped up one dark evening to watch the sky. Negative results, apart from a bit of rain. But my enthusiasm for the subject was never knowingly dampened and this inevitably lead me to the delightful Wiltshire town of Warminster. Now Warminster, during the 1960s, had apparently, a non-stop parade of strange aerial objects flitting about with seeming gay abandon. I delved further. High in the Warminster UFO firmament was a local West Country journalist named Arthur Shuttlewood. And so it goes after an alleged bout of scepticism, Arthur nailed firmly his reporting skills to the worldwide interest in the Warminster Flying Saucer or 'Thing' as it was dubbed. Arthur became a convert to the cause. He was an engaging and garrulous individual and he expounded, to anyone who would listen, an entirely plausible case for the entire Flying Saucer phenomenon. He did this at regular intervals, usually to a small but rapt audience, all waiting to get a word in edgeways. His entertaining book, *The Warminster Mystery* became an immediate bestseller.

I had never seen a UFO and so in 1967 I travelled to Warminster in the hope of revelations. I took along my 16mm Bolex movie camera to make a 'sky watch' film about, (as it transpired), a group of people wandering around on a hill, not seeing a UFO. My film was called *The Warminster Watch*. It was shown later to a packed audience at the Caxton Hall in London (a rather scratched copy can now be viewed on YouTube) and it featured Arthur and chums waving telescopes and 'UFO detectors' across the Wiltshire skyline in the hope of seeing the elusive 'Thing'. Local landmark Cradle Hill was the sky watching hot spot, but no spots, hot or otherwise, were seen. A local BBC Television crew arrived to cover the event, and later I distinctly heard the cameraman mutter to his producer that we were all 'a bunch of bloody loonies'.

With that endorsement ringing in my ears, my next close encounter with UFOs was on a fan discussion panel at a science fiction convention. I was inveigled to sit on this panel and found myself next to author Michael Moorcock, an imposing, opinionated and popular writer of science fiction. Sitting alongside a few others (offering no support I might add) there was lonely old me up there to argue the case of 'Why Flying Saucers?' This was the panel title, listed in the programme of Convention Events.

Me and Mr Moorcock. Cartoon scratched on a stencil for a Fanzine. It was all done by hand in the olden days.

I came armed with notes, evidence and other bits and bobs to convince the sceptic. At the last moment I couldn't find them, which didn't help the nervous twitch I had developed during the course of the morning. Mike Moorcock spread his colours early, adopting his characteristic reasoned approach. 'Mass hysteria,' he opined, 'War psychosis,' he added, a phrase he had pinched from the Russians. 'People don't *really* see flying saucers, they're worried about the Vietnam war.' The rest of the panel mumbled in agreement. I was outnumbered. I looked again for my notes. 'It's a chain reaction you see,' Mike continued. 'People read about UFOs in the paper and then go out and *imagine* they see them.' I was asked for my opinion. 'I believe in the existence of space machines from other worlds,' I cried, 'Why not? What is wrong with that admission?' Well *everything*, according to Mike. 'War psychosis,' he reiterated. 'The largest amounts of sightings occur when the population is concerned about its personal safety. People are worried about the Bomb too.' At that point I lapsed into a resigned silence. Understandable, when the rest of the panel, plus the formidable Mike Moorcock, had such cut and dried explanations to parry with. Besides I needed time to reflect upon my newly acquired war psychosis.

No Sarge.. not Little Green **MEN!**

Feeling a Touch Crabby Today

It was now 1971 and I was drifting along with quite a few published cartoons and also a few strips. Yes, I had made the small time at last! Several weekly and monthly efforts including, *Hi Fi Hector* in a Hi Fi magazine *Video Vic* in a video magazine and *Movie Millie –Queen of the Hard "Cors"* in a very rude magazine (but more of that later). Another strip, *Office Hours* ran for a few years in an industry trade magazine (for the computer fraternity) called *Datalink*. I've added this to the list because my wife Margaret supplied me with themes for this strip. Indeed she *appears* in it! The 'office' in question was the IT department of a lightly disguised City stockbroker firm called Phillips & Drew where Margaret was employed as a computer programmer. Nobody twigged (or cared) but the strip ran for quite a few years and it was good money too.

During 1971, we bid farewell to South Croydon. Margaret and myself scraped together a deposit, enough towards an £8,000 mortgage (oh, the good old days) and bought an end of terrace three-bedroomed town house in Chelmsford, Essex. Why Chelmsford? Draw a circle on a map and work outwards taking note of property prices. Bit cheaper the further the circle spread. Which brings me to CRAB.

Now, CRAB was the Chelmsford Radical Bulletin (whose acronym should have actually been CRB). Anyway, my involvement began when I visited the opticians for an eye check and new specs. I was obliged to give my occupation, 'Ah, a cartoonist eh?' said Maurice the optician, 'Just what we need!' Oh goody thought I, as I envisaged working for some lucrative glossy optician's trade rag. But no, that was not the case. It appeared that Maurice the optician was a spare-time leftie who worked with a group of similar-minded activists, producing a small publication with very radical tendencies. 'We have meetings every month', Maurice the optician continued. 'Do come along. I'm sure you will be able to help us.' As I had just moved into the area and was feeling a little isolated, I agreed to come along, if only to meet some new people. 'We need some cartoons to jolly our magazine up a bit,' Maurice the optician remarked on parting. So, as promised the following week I attended the meeting, held in an upstairs room, next to the town hall. I was greeted by several baggy trousered revolutionaries and their Molls, straight from Central Casting. Ten people in all, of which it transpired, *eight* were the collective 'editor' of this radical magazine, known to very few as CRAB. I was shown a copy of the magazine, (the one needing jollificating). It was explained that CRAB was produced each month with the benefit of a true Democratic Ideal.

'This is Fred, he writes the editorial. This is Monica, she sub-edits the editorial. This is Gilbert he proof-reads the editorial. This is Eric he re-writes the editorial... and this is Jo. She organized our 'Sack Thatcher The Milk Snatcher' protest march last year, and she was eight months pregnant at the time'. I didn't enquire as to whether her pregnancy was the outcome of a true Democratic Editorial Ideal.

So I sat in the corner of the room for the rest of the evening and listened to heated polemic. The magazine got scant attention until, right at the end, a decision was taken to discuss the next issue. A motion was then passed to the effect that in future, all editorial meetings would discuss the magazine. This all seemed reasonable to me, a mere newcomer to radical thought. And then I was unanimously voted in as paste-up, layout and general magazine artist. The ensemble was visibly relieved, when I unconditionally accepted the post, not so much because of my undoubted skill at magazine work but more because none of the collective assembled political geniuses considered the task of layout and paste up a fitting job for the architects of the New Britain. I took a copy of CRAB magazine home with me to study.

What an utter shambles it was. Home-duplicated on a knackered litho machine. Over and under inked on the same page. Print through, smudges, typos, the lot! This poor excuse for a magazine was actually on sale at five pence. Not surprisingly, sales were very low. About two hundred copies were printed, half distributed to a local factory and the rest found their sorry way into a few shops, or hand-distributed in the shopping precinct. Sales were falling every month. It now dawned on me that I had been roped in to jazz up the magazine's pitiful appearance in the wild hope that it would improve its chances in the market place. However, it was never apparent to our motley collection of Trotskyists, Maoists, Commies and Co-operatives that it was the *message* not the medium that was anathema to the citizens of Chelmsford town. However, I was eager to please, full of plans, roughs, typefaces, gate-folds and cartoons.

At the next editorial meeting all heads, if not hearts, turned in my direction. I proceeded to display my fresh and gleaming Letraset-ed proof copy of the new, redder than red CRAB. It proved a success and I started as paste-up artist that very night. The plates had been booked at a local printer for the following day, but you can't impress the need for a deadline on a den of dreamers and at CRAB, I had eight to deal with.

The evening chugged on and still nothing had arrived at my corner. Across the room a woman sat typing the various offerings for me to paste up, but no sooner had she finished one sheet, it was then pounced upon by one of the 'editors' and 'edited' and then another 'editor' 'edited' the 'edits' and so on around the room. This absurd situation persisted until, in desperation, I grabbed at the pages as they left the typewriter in order to get anything at all stuck down. Once it took three hours to decide whether a 'Coming Events' item should be included. By the time they had decided, no doubt the event had gone.

I had reserved the back page of the magazine for a Dicky Howett cartoon. My cartoon was not specifically political. No Capitalist in a top hat and tails bashing a dungaree-clad loon on the bonce with a sack of South African gold. My cartoon (and others in the magazine) were social comments targeting the failings of petty officialdom and the like. I thought that the general readership would appreciate the injection of local flavour, but our gang of eight had other ideas.

After every issue of CRAB, the public were invited to attend a meeting with the express purpose of criticizing the issue and offering suggestions. Only the editors and their friends ever seemed to turn up, but the exercise was never considered pointless. After a few praises and grumbles about minor points, my layout was generally approved until an unidentified individual stood up and wanted to know why the Howett cartoons were funny. He was not seeking an intellectual discourse on humour, he was just puzzled that humour should be used so freely in a political journal. 'I don't like all this funny stuff' he concluded. I sat stunned. Where am I? thought I. Then one of the editors, a snivelling gnome of an individual I had never really taken to, suddenly agreed with the questioner. He too had disliked my cartoons but had kept quiet for the sake of unity. And after all the hours I had spent sticking down their juvenile rantings! Then the rest of the ungrateful mob joined in and condemned me as a revisionist, whatever that was. It got all quite hectic.

I was understandably mortified at this incredible outburst, being quite unused to such displays of hostility and criticism. I seriously considered the possibility that there was something wrong with me. I hadn't known at the time that this kind of brain bashing was a regular feature of these 'readers meetings', all designed to deflate the ego and root out a cult of personality. My cartoons apparently had too much ego (*i.e.* 'me') in them. But I didn't understand this at the time and got all huffy and left. I was waylaid at the door by one sympathetic editor who explained this 'ego' business and tried to persuade me to return. But it was obvious that I was not suited to the cause. In fact, I could never have abided or accepted the strictures of such a witless bunch, who so misunderstood the criteria of humour or were so negligent of the desires of the public they so desperately wanted to convert. The committee had wanted me to jolly their magazine up but in the end they proved they couldn't decide on anything, apart for discontinuing the magazine that is.

Ever the glutton for punishment, a year or two later, I teamed with journalist chum Jo Gable and we became briefly 'non-political' press barons. We devised and published a local newspaper called *The Chelmsford Independent*, a sort of regional consumer guide featuring *exposé* and general tattle. Naturally, this was not welcomed with open arms by local businesses. Our feature articles tended to criticize various pubs (sample text: '*The Running Mare's toilets had Running Mould*'), plus price comparisons at local supermarkets and the low down on, for example, bad dentists or council planning follies *etc.* Our 'hit list' was naively endless. But to our surprise, our first issue sold out! At least we thought it had. Unfortunately it was not to be. It transpired we had sold hardly any copies, due mainly to our faithless local 'distributor' neglecting to distribute copies. A big pile of issue number one was found in his warehouse hiding under a big box. The main local newspaper (or so we believed) had exerted a little pressure. Live and learn. Ho-hum.

Around that time, the town of Chelmsford decided to hold an Arts Festival and local artists were invited to apply for space to display their works. The 'space' was the railings down by the River Chelmer' (a fetid stream which runs sluggishly through the town centre). In eager anticipation, I pinned up my stuff and awaited sales. Well, let's face it who had ever heard of me? No sales all day, until at last, my next door neighbour took pity and bought a cartoon. Needn't have bothered really.

Look East Young Man

Throughout the 1970s I was producing many highly specialized single cartoons for several bottom-of-the-pile, but top-of-the-shelf publications with titles such as *Sexy Laffs* and *Ribald Rudies*. No prizes for guessing the subject matter. I became quite adept at one-frame 'funny' smut, sometimes actually featuring bottoms and piles. I was churning out the stuff, and selling it at a phenomenal rate (a phenomenal rate, incidentally, that worked out at one pound per cartoon). Not riches untold to be sure, but all this proved to be an open drain into which I remorselessly tipped my wit. My cartoons covered the entire spectrum of sexuality (this was in the pre-PC days before certain themes were shunned or frowned upon). My dirty work was in great demand and I soon moved upmarket to *Men Only*, *Knave*, *Club International*, *Mayfair* and *Penthouse*. At one stroke I jumped from a one pound rate to a forty pound rate per cartoon, many drawn in full colour too.

During that period I became a member of the National Union Of Journalists which was pushing for, believe it or not, a closed shop for all us pro cartoonists (CRAB had a lot to answer for). During one of our interminable NUJ meetings I was approached by journalist Anna Coote and in the course of our chat, Coote mooted a theme for an article she was considering for the *Guardian* newspaper. Something along the lines of man's sexual expression in an increasingly dehumanizing society... or how sexist sex cartoonists earn a living (I hasten to add Ms Coote did not find me particularly sexist, nor indeed sexy for that matter). The *Guardian* liked the proposal and the article was duly published later in the *Guardian* Women's page.

When it finally appeared, Coote's article, although entertaining and erudite, proved innocuous and rather inconclusive. Covering themes such as Donald McGill and naughty seaside postcards, later it described me as 'a mild and pleasant young man' an epithet more appropriate for a brand of milk stout than a highly talented cartoonist! The article as published, and my comments, seemed rather at odds as to what I remember saying. I recalled that Ms Coote and I spent a relaxing afternoon at my Chelmsford abode, covering many aspects of the cartoon trade and my aspirations within it. Okay, so I might have embellished things a bit. Not exactly *lying* but to be honest, most of it was quite near the truth. In the event and in glaring newsprint, I presented myself for all the world to see as a first rate opinionated pillock. Thus I vowed in future to purport myself with all due caution and veracity. I didn't have long to wait for my resolution to be put to the test.

The day after Anna Coote's article appeared, I received a phone call from an assistant at the production office of BBC television's *Look East* which was (and still is) an Eastern regional programme transmitted early evenings from that fine city of Norwich. The assistant said that they had read Ms Coote's little item and as Chelmsford was just about within the East Anglian boundaries, I qualified for an appearance on the show. I agreed instantly, neglecting altogether to remember my vow of veracity and non-pillockness. It seemed like another golden opportunity to make things up and this time on TV! The assistant said they would arrange to send a film crew the following week. The crew arrived at the appointed day but they were very late. I had planned to take them over to my allotment with me 'digging' around for ideas, a sort of visual pun. But it was now too dark and so, to make the best of it, we were all crammed into my office. The director was quite scruffy looking and he wore a creased suit and a puzzled air. He explained they had just come from filming haddock at Harwich and were not quite sure why they were here. 'I got this call on my radio car phone, see. They said come down here. What do you suggest we do?' queried the director.

Oh dear, wrong question. So there they were, a full BBC crew, Director, Cameraman, Lighting Engineer, Sound Engineer and a woman interviewer, Australian if I recall, all waiting for me to invent something. I suggested rude cartoons, but that was quite out of the question, pre-watershed and all that. Thus we agreed to concoct a sort of local 'Look at Life', or 'How a Cartoonist Works In His Home With His Family There To Support Him'. A captivating theme to be sure.

Then we set about planning a totally scripted, spontaneous interview. The Aussie lady interviewer seemed in a bit of a dream and she spent most of the prep time staring fixedly at my crotch (my flared trousers *were* extremely tight in those far off days). Eventually we finalized some questions and ripostes with a selection of my cartoons pinned to the wall to use as cutaways. All I had to do was remember a few key words during the interview so that later, the film editor could splice in a shot of the relevant cartoon. Things started smoothly enough. I sketched a cartoon 'on camera' explaining to the viewing thousands what I was doing and then adding the punch line at the end. To the manner born, thought I. Then things started going wrong. I began forgetting the script and for some inexplicable reason my mind wandered to the camera with all that expensive Eastman colour film stock racing through the gate at 25 frames per second. Hurry, hurry, say anything! And than I heard myself spouting utter cobblers about how my favourite cartoonist was Carl Giles (not) and how I wanted to be a political cartoonist (not) and how my three year old daughter Lucy gave me lots of ideas for cartoons (never). Magic words to the director, because that meant now a link to the 'family situation' and the camera was moved to my living room with my cute offspring grizzling in the corner. Lucy steadfastly refused to perform on camera. No amount of cajoling made any difference. Kids have a nose for bullshitters.

Eventually the director announced a 'wrap'. He seemed pleased with everything. 'Ron got some nice shots of your hand drawing,' he said. 'We can easily cut all this down to six minutes.' I expressed disbelief. I mean, to start with, one of my sentences was at least six minutes long and then there was all that stuff with my pens and inks and sharpening pencils not to mention my Eagle comic collection. But no, things were just fine and dandy. 'We'll let you know when it's transmitted,' the director said as they left, 'they may even pay.' Actually, I had been meaning to ask them to cough up for the electricity they used (the lamps were very bright) but thought better of it. I was hoping for a repeat performance and didn't want to spoil my chances. They never did pay.

Two weeks later, when the interview was transmitted, it shone as a masterpiece of artifice. My snivelling brat was transformed into a golden commercial for washing-up liquid, sitting attentively at my wife's side and giggling as her famous daddy read her a comic. I remember that bit, that was after I dragged her into the bathroom and threatened to dismember her rag doll. Her film giggles were probably stifled hysteria. But the greatest revelation was of 'Dicky Howett TV Star and his voice'. Gone was my imagined deep masculine well-modulated bass. Instead, erupting from the TV set was a curious whiny chirruping tone plus lots of sniffing. But nobody else seemed aware of this and my performance was praised by friends and for a short time, neighbours pointed at me in the street. I had recorded my performance on an audio tape and clicked a few snaps off the screen (the days before VHS video) but as with most transmitted stuff, my specific TV appearance had vanished into the cosmos, never to be viewed again... Or had it?

Let us scroll forward eighteen-or-so years. By the 1990s I was supplementing my cartoon work by writing media-related articles for several niche publications (*What Video*, *Camcorder User*, *Complete CD* and so on). I was commissioned by one to write a series about film and TV archiving. This lead me to the East Anglia Film Archive, established in 1976 and based at the University Of East Anglia near Norwich. Curator of the archive was David Cleveland whom, incidentally, I had worked at the BBC's Ealing Studios projection department way back in 1964. David was keen to publicize the archive which, at the time, housed over 14,000 items, preserved on all film gauges, 8mm, Super 8, 9.5mm, 16mm, 28mm and 35mm. Video tape was stored in a special 'magnetic free' vault. During our interview David told me that he was in the process of acquiring and storing all of the film footage from BBC East with the eventual purpose of preserving the entire regional back catalogue. Perhaps then my 1975 *Look East* 16mm colour interview was saved and could I see it? Sorry no, BBC East had junked everything prior to 1976. It transpired that when the *Look East* 'Film Library' shelf got filled, they would chuck out the oldest cans to make room for new items. Brilliant scheme. Thanks, BBC.

Supermum Does a Spot of Clubbing

On the Dec 1st 1977 along came *Supermum*. This full-page, twelve-frame strip was featured in IPC's *Whoopee!* comic and it was my very first attempt drawing for the kiddies humour market. At the time, Bob Paynter was the editor and it is to him I owe my 'break'. Bob confessed later, in his cups, that he thought I was going to be one of the best children's cartoonists in the UK. Unfortunately, prophecy wasn't one of Bob's stronger points.

Supermum, or Margie Mussels to give her real name, was a sort of high-speed super heroic Old Mother Riley. Super-mum resided in a town called 'Chelmsditch'. I am nothing if not original because her environment closely resembled my home town of Chelmsford. She had a son called Terry and a monosyllabic husband who was seen usually slumped in an armchair uttering 'Umms', 'Ooohs' and the occasional 'YIKE!' when Supermum shifted his chair suddenly or sneezed.

The *Supermum* strip had originally been offered to a well-known singles cartoonist called Styx (Vic Sarkans). He had attempted a treatment but felt unable to develop it further for publication. Apparently he couldn't instil the characters with the necessary whoosh, zip and blam!, the vibrancy of kids cartoons.

I was not at all confident when the strip was offered to me. I had never undertaken a weekly full-page cartoon strip before, but at least my single cartoons showed a degree of movement which is, I suppose, why the editor chose me. I did quite well.

Within a year *Supermum* had gained so much popularity (via votes submitted) that it was decided to 'run a competition'. Enter the great 'Win- a-T-shirt' contest. The winnable T-shirts were hand-painted (special iron-on stuff) by me. I did ten and was paid £100. My daughter Lucy and I were photographed for publicity purposes at IPC wearing a selection of these T-Shirts and in a very short time, the editorial staff waded through over 1000 eager entries, which, I was told, was something of a record.

To win a T-shirt the kids had to draw their own versions of *Supermum* and the best submissions won. I saw some of these pictures and they were quite illuminating and touching. Several kids had, alarmingly, copied my style exactly, even down to my signature! Kids miss nothing, but nothing. Hector the Worm joined quite soon after. I began adding him to the page as a sort of invertebrate Greek Chorus. One example had him dressed in dark glasses and a pastry case. 'I'm a mince-spy' he shrieked. Once, I drew a hole in the ground with a small notice which read, 'the worm's on holiday'. As a variation I would sometimes incorporate Hector in the design of one of the panels. He was perhaps, shaped like a cloud, a finger, or a dog's tail (nothing risqué of course). The readers then had to hunt for him, with the answer revealed in the letters page. Very useful this, as it enabled me to discover where I hid the bloody thing. I drew the strip two months on advance and I couldn't usually remember where I had hidden the worm. Kids, naturally, found him instantly!

I actually took *Supermum* on holiday. In those days we took three weeks family vacation on the small Channel Island of Alderney. Three weeks of relentless holiday fun can get a bit tedious and I was getting slightly bored by the end of it. So one year I carted my pens and inks with me. I had the scripts so I spent some evenings completing artwork. Dedication or what? I even did a cartoon or two for the *Alderney Newspaper* which is about as small scale as you can get. Readership in the handfuls. Back from holidays, I was on a roll. My 'comic' drawing style was unconventional (*i.e.* not based on the 1930s pattern) but I would be the first to admit that the style I adopted was not particularly appealing.

However, I felt I was improving all the time. Incidentally, all the strip's lettering was done in-house. All I had to do was leave sufficient spaces for the text. This was okay by me because my graphic skills were no great shakes as well as a bit shaky. Fellow cartoonist and Supermum scriptwriter Roy Davis once criticized me for not being able to draw a convincing cartoon gorilla. He was absolutely justified because my simian attempt looked curiously like a hairy Benny Hill. Roy used to submit his *Supermum* scripts in the form of a full-page rough with all the panels sketched out. I could have just copied the lot, he was that good.

Continued on back page...

Typical Supermum. Good enough for the front covers.
No extra money though.

Drawing or devising cartoons all day was, for me, a solitary business. A little light relief needed perhaps? The Cartoonists Club Of Great Britain (which, I believe still exists, the Club not Great Britain, although that might be the case in the future). Anyway, back to the past. I joined the Club in the early 1970s and looked forward each month to the regular monthly meetings held in a pub just off Shoe Lane. The pub was named The Cartoonist and several of us would spend a convivial evening trying to match our *nom de plumes* with our actual names and visages. I always signed myself as 'Dicky Howett' but some cartoonists hid behind oddities such as 'Naylor' (James Gubb) 'Quanda' (Frank Holmes) or 'Belespot' (Allen King). If those are unfamiliar, grander figures sometimes graced the pub, Bill Tidy, Terry Parkes (Larry), Frank Dickens, John Burns, Kipper Williams, even the great Frank Hampson (although as a Club member he never, to my knowledge, visited).

Cartoonists on a jolly. Butlin's at Pwiiheli 1978ish
Our annual cartoonist family get together. Our club's President
was Sir Billy Butlin so a cheap time was had by all.

It was pleasure also to meet Denis Gifford, that pre-eminent collector and font of all things Comic. He always gave me encouragement, and indeed he commissioned me to draw a full page strip cartoon for his wonderful *Ally Sloper* magazine (the final issue as it transpired). Denis was working on a popular Thames TV show called *Quick On The Draw* (1974-1979) which featured Bob Monkhouse and Bill Tidy being witty with a pen, plus a bunch of guest 'comedians' who couldn't draw a line and weren't much funnier. Denis tried several times to get me on the show, but as luck would have it, when it looked as if I might at last have been invited to perform, the programme got cancelled.

I mentioned the signing of names to cartoons. On one occasion I ducked out of being Dicky Howett and became instead, 'Dave Richards', this for an exemplar gay monthly magazine called *Jeremy* (1969) billed as 'The Magazine For Modern Young Men'. The magazine had been devised and commissioned by a personable fashion photographer called Peter Marriott. He had had the inspiration for a timely glossy men's magazine and had somehow considered yours truly as suitable for the post of Art Editor, Paste Up Artist, General Illustrator and Cartoonist. Thus, I set about designing themes and styles, aided and abetted by my bemused wife Margaret and liberal quantities of Letraset. Along the way, I proposed a humorous strip entitled *James Blond: The Randy Dandy With The Handy Pandy*. This strip contained extremely sophisticated repartee which included James Blond announcing that he 'got where he was by starting at the 'bottom'.

I roped in chum Christopher Priest as 'Features Director: 'Richard Harrington' and Chris provided some excellent short story and other text material. The 48-page magazine (which looked very classy, if I say so myself, I even thought up the magazine's name) had film reviews, cooking, fiction, cartoons, a horoscope called 'Heavenly Bodies' and many fashion images. Peter Marriott advertised this magazine (in *Private Eye* amongst others) on the basis of subscription, or direct sale only. It was never intended as WH Smith top-shelf material. Soon, the postal orders (six shillings a copy) came flooding in. What killed the magazine (after one issue) was twofold. Remember, the Sexual Offences Act had only been on the statute books for two years, and (although it was still the Swinging Sixties, just), the moral minority 'Festival Of Light' brigade could have found any old excuse to prosecute. Why? Well it was never put to the test, (because Peter quickly withdrew the magazine from sale), but perhaps an object of complaint could have been of a nudist image, (quite innocuous), showing a full-frontal teenage boy on a beach? And another of a teenaged boy in y-fronts (fashion section). However, as far as I was concerned, the other, more pertinent reason for ditching the magazine was that I never got paid my full fee of £200. Nuff said.

After that small stumble, my cartoon career progressed. Apart from dear old *Supermum*, I drew further feature strips for 'in-house' magazines including for a firm of risk assessors. So what, you may well ask, is funny about risk assessment? Very little, to be honest and even less for another trade magazine aimed at pharmacists, where themes tackling pile pills or condoms need extremely careful handing to avoid descending into the lewd. Other interesting work arrived including designing a brochure for expectant mothers, and another for microwave ovens ('Instant Kitchens'. Yet another unpaid account, still awaiting the £25, mate!).

And then the BBC entered again. In all honesty the corporation never really left my life and hasn't yet. During the 1970s I had acquired an agent. Her name was Janet Freer and occasionally she found unusual assignments for me. Although primarily a literary agent, I believe she took me on as a novelty side-line. On one occasion, she asked me to attend a recording at Lime Grove studio G. Nothing spectacular, just a BBC training exercise for a tyro TV director called Martin Everard. The director, as part of his training remit, had to mount a 'real' programme. His idea was called *7 Up* which was an early venture into breakfast TV. This was way before actual breakfast television appeared to delight us all. I had two spots on the show where I sat at my easel and drew some topical cartoons. Of my performance I have no real memory apart from, during rehearsal, hearing the director screaming (a cameraman's headset was turned up full) to get me to 'start his bloody scene'. I had misheard my cue and had waited in silence whilst the camera homed in. I should have been talking away when the camera homed in. No praise for me there then. The director did later confess he had tried to get Bill Tidy to take part but got me instead.

An exhibit at the London Tate Gallery. (No, not me) The exhibition featured a collection of published cartoons (not the originals-enlarged copies) with the theme of 'a child of six could do it' referring to modern art. My little effort had an artist hanging on a frame (top right) saying..'and then I thought, what can I put in the exhibition this year..? My cartoon had been published originally in The Daily Mirror. The era of long hair and tank tops.

Enter the Mighty Marvel Quinn

I first encountered a certain individual called Quinn at a convention for comic artists and writers. This was Strips 78 held at the Y hotel, just off Tottenham Court Road in London. The convention was one of Denis Gifford's little enterprises, held for no discernible reason. The place itself was full of cartoonists and guests. During a fag break I was approached by a diffident and unassuming character. He announced himself as a certain Tim Quinn and professed to be an avid fan of my work. He said also that he wrote scripts for D.C. Thomson and in particular *Dennis the Menace*. We soon got into a discussion about, mainly the poor state of British comics (in hindsight, a continuing moan of ours). I suggested to Tim (more to cheer him up really) that he submit a few scripts for my strip Supermum and this he duly did. I really thought no more of it. To be honest, I didn't fancy the idea of *Supermum* becoming another D.C. Dennis. But my doubts proved unfounded, because Tim's scripts (once they had been filtered through editor, Bob Paynter) were a breath of fresh air, full of originality and invention and importantly, funny! At last the 1930s had been left behind! It was now time to cook with gas!

Later, Tim had an idea for a feature entitled *The Gold Rush*. This strip, (cunningly designed to last forever) had two loony lads rushing around the entire globe competing and searching for an inheritance. We both took the idea to Bob Paynter, but as we all drifted up in the lift at IPC's formidable Kings Reach Tower HQ, Tim announced suddenly to Bob and myself that 'Tim and Dicky' had won an American Best Cartoon Team Of The Year contest. Perhaps Tim was feeling particularly insecure at the time, but I just nodded and concurred at this Quinn comic book fiction and hastily changed the subject before the lift doors opened. This fanciful 'award' of Tim's was never ever mentioned again.

Supermum d a s h e d on until the end of 1981 when, for reasons unknown, it was peremptorily cancelled. The strip itself was highly popular and throughout its run, appeared in many Summer Specials and even graced the front cover of *Whoopee Comic* several times. *The Gold Rush* strip had finished a year earlier and now I was left with no IPC comic work at all. Tim and I pushed a few ideas but nothing appealed. I did have the inkling of a suspicion that my adult cartoon work was somehow influencing the editors and their decisions to dump me. But hey ho, and onward. Tim had suggested earlier that we contact a strange little outfit based in the North London suburb of Kentish Town. This was Marvel Comics UK and thus when one door closes... about ten others open.

Ten. I think that was about the number of weekly Marvel magazines that Tim and myself had our cartoons published in. It seems barely credible, but back at the beginning of the 1980s, Marvel UK (or MUK as it was known, affectionately) was out to conquer the UK specialist comic magazine market. Reprints of *Spider-man*, *The Incredible Hulk*, or *The Mighty Thor* were cleverly re-packaged as the *Marvel Super Hero* series, attractive and competitively priced.

Tim's initial jolly Marvel idea was called *I Was Adolf's Double*. As the title suggests, it was a rollicking World War Two adventure featuring a bunch of fun-loving Nazis and an innocent Ramsgate gardener called Winston S. Quaill, who was Hitler's eponymous double. There was bit of initial trouble with Winston's surname. Tim had wanted to call him 'Cohen', but editor Paul Neary scrubbed that and replaced it with 'Quaill', which made no sense to us. We didn't argue, being Marvel new boys. We were just relived to have found a seemingly receptive market for our work.

I spent many delightful hours sketching the world's pre-eminent genocidal maniacs in a comical, but at the same time, deeply unflattering light. I had noticed in the old newsreels that Goebbels was a cripple who walked like a wonky pigeon so I made him a dwarf and gave him great pointy feet. Hermann Goering was depicted as a loud-mouthed fat git and Lord HawHaw, the traitorous radio correspondent was portrayed as a Rolls Royce-riding, top hatted, manacled upper class tit, don't cha know.

The series ran for 15 weeks in *Forces In Combat* and it was only recently that I discovered a small and, in retrospect, a totally crass joke that I had innocently inserted into one of the frames. As was my practice, I habitually embellished Tim's scripts with visual puns. Part 12 of the series began with a 'Berlin High Strasse' scene and on a vacant lot, 'The Reichstag Nazi Gang Hut'. On the wall next to the hut was a poster which read 'Non-Aryans Welcome at Billy Belsen's Holiday Camp'.

A few years later the entire 15 week run of *Adolf* was reprinted in our one-off Summer Special Marvel publication, *Channel 33⅓ The Children's Comic TV Station*. My holocaust holiday camp reference was never commented upon. What *did* get up somebody's nose was all the allusions to glue sniffing, prostitution and fornication. An irate parent had imagined seeing all this in our Special, enough to complain loudly to the editors and threaten prosecution. Copies of the magazine were sent to the Metropolitan police, but nothing ever came of it. Tim and myself were thus fortunately spared the prospect of having to while away our 'time' devising humorous prison news sheets for fellow inmates.

Tim's next jolly idea was a three-frame strip cartoon satirizing all of Marvel's superheroes. We called the strip *Earth 33⅓*. My inspiration and model for the format was a similar series running in the USA by a cartoonist called Fred Hembeck. In my arrogance, I thought I could do much better. In all honesty I really struggled to characterize the Marvel Super Heroes. Some of my drawings of the Marvel Super lads and lassies were almost recognizable. These strips, which we churned out (daily it seemed), appeared across the entire Marvel weekly comic range. I was not then (or now) in any way a Marvel Super Hero fan, nor indeed a comic book reader. I had no real understanding what or whom I was drawing, but like a true professional I just blagged my way through and stuck it out, if only for the money.

Which brings us to *Jet Lagg: The Fastest Slowcoach In The Galaxy*. This was our next feature strip for Marvel and Tim and I had high hopes for this one. Jet Lagg's first adventure had him, and sidekick, the curiously named *Spunky*, battling with a clockwork Ayatollah doll and a giant Margaret Thatcher. This, to us, seemed a reasonable collection of villains (after all it was the innocent 1980s) but no, Mr Editor hit heads and we had to change things. Any reference to an Ayatollah got scrubbed and Thatcher became *Queen Kong*. Upon publication, the observant might have noticed some hastily drawn hair on Thatcher's face but otherwise she still looked very much like the old hand-bagging milk-snatcher we all knew and loved.

But nevertheless, undaunted by incomprehensible editorial directives, we plugged away at Marvel UK and offered even more humorous feature strips. *The Fairly Amazing Spider Hound* (who attained his powers by being bitten by a radioactive flea) and *The Fantastic 400 (new reprint edition now available!)* which a gleeful Tim negligently foisted on me. This meant I now had to draw at least 400 new characters, usually in the same frame, and I did! Even later, for an American child's magazine he adapted *The Fantastic 400* and transformed it into *The Fitness 500*! Thanks Tim

Another prize character was *Hulk The Menace*, an exquisite combination of Dennis the Menace and The Incredible Hulk. Tim imbued *Hulk The Menace* with all the attributes he had been denied when scripting the vapid D.C. Thomson *Dennis*. This new improved Hulk-type Dennis now ate copious quantities of baked beans and farted for all he was worth. That was all okay. Nothing wrong with a good honest honk. What was *not* okay was the depiction of the Hulk Hooligan Party. Politics again, so

59

they had to be careful I suppose. *Hulk The Menace* was standing as his own Hooligan candidate, but this was way too much for Marvel. It was election year in the UK, and the editors decided that *H.T.M.* might influence voters with his decidedly loony tune views. I drew up the three 'election' themed scripts, numbers 57, 58 and 59 and submitted the finished artwork, but those three were never published. There was quite a nice caricature of BBC interviewer Robin Day in there too. Oh, and a TV camera...

Tim and myself were quite a prolific team during the 1980s. Our combined efforts appeared in a multiplicity of magazines. One such was a strip aimed at video game fans (*TV Gamer*). We also approached regional posh county magazines such as *Essex Countryside*, who published our little pseudo local histories written by Tim, and bedecked with my apposite illustrations. We also contributed to a Fan Aid charity magazine, this about the time of the Geldof funfest at Wembley. But, as we now considered ourselves to be a top flight cartooning team, we became less charitable towards 'bloody editors', who were certainly getting under our collective skins. So we thought: here's an idea, let's be our *own* editors! Simps.

Is it a Dummy or is it Noel?

It seemed a jolly good wheeze: Cut out the top bozo and edit to our own taste. A comic for the 1980s at last! It was apparent that I couldn't realistically draw the entire thing, and so I contacted a few of the top British comic artists to see if they would contribute artwork (free) for a dummy issue. The response was gratifying. I got swift replies from the cream including David Lloyd, Ed McHenry, Nick Baker, Nigel Edwards, Jim Barker and the peerless Ron Tiner. With the finished artwork in place, I assembled the dummy issue which we named *ZIP!* and began the usual soul destroying process of hawking the wares. Unbeknownst to me, Tim had decided (upon advice) to create a 'news item press release'. One of *ZIP!*'s strips was entitled *The Devil Wants You* and a frame showed some skin heads (under the influence of 'The Devil') on the rampage and in another, a man was shown attempting to murder his wife. Simple, warm-hearted kids stuff you will agree. This dastardly product was picked up by, amongst others, lovely old ITN. (they 'fell' for the bogus news item). I was in London at the time delivering some artwork to *TV Gamer* magazine. Whilst in the office I made a phone call Tim, (a query or something). Tim suddenly informed me that ITN had just recorded an interview with him 'down the line' and it was to be broadcast on the ITN one o'clock news. What was all this all about then, I pondered.

As ITN's Wells Street studios were but a short stroll from the *TV Gamer* office, at noon, I ambled in and identified myself, asking if I could kindly watch the broadcast from the foyer? To whit I was whisked straight into the studio and plonked next to Leonard Parkin. 'You can do the interview' they told me.

So cue Leonard with me sitting clueless beside him, waiting to be asked questions about what, I didn't know exactly. I must have mumbled something reasonably comprehensible because soon, the interview was over and Leonard graciously thanked me. A nice man. Afterwards in the green room I met some more TV faces and showed them a few of my cartoons. Agreeable afternoon. Got paid thirty pounds too. A very brief fragment of VHS recording exists, (a friend suddenly recognised me) and he punched the record button, rather too late to catch much. But for all that careful media manipulation, our *ZIP!* comic sank before it had even started, never to see the light of day again. I still have all the wonderful dummy artwork.

After the absolute total failure to interest any print publisher, Tim and I re-imagined and retitled *ZIP! as ARGH!*. For this we approached the various television companies to try and enthuse them in a TV series about cartoons and comics featuring, naturally, Tim and Dicky as the writers and star presenters. I cobbled together a nice little illustrated *ARGH!* prospectus which we brandished around the various TV production offices. The initial spark was the imminent arrival of cable television. The 1980s had been a time of deregulation and Cable Laying was flavour of the decade. Tim had assumed that nascent cable TV companies would be crying out for material (not true at all) but we began big by approaching the national broadcasters, like Channel 4 and Granada and then reduced our expectations down to regional companies like TVS and Anglia.

Tim and I traipsed around the studios and at one of them a commissioning editor (for TVS) kept asking us continually *why* we wanted to present a TV show about comics. I had not the balls to reply, 'because I want to be fucking famous and earn lots of cash, chum!' Rejections didn't stop us. Give us an excuse and we would contact any old outlet that would have us. Later, our two cartoon books, the *Doctor Who Fun Book* and *It's Bigger On The Inside* set us off on a round of frenzied promotions: Liverpool, (Granada) Leeds, (YTV) Norwich, (Anglia TV). Local radio even, perhaps not the best medium to promote a purely visual product, but hey, we were in the spotlight again and did we love it!

Our first major television appearance was in 1980, when we convinced the mighty BBC that Quinn and Howett really ought to be on the small screen. Marvel UK had just produced a 'science fiction' magazine called *Future Tense* which included our latest cartoon offering *The Concise History of the Galaxy*, not a million miles from a sort of *Hitchhiker's Guide*. A notable feature in our 'history' was that it didn't have a paranoid android but instead, a peripatetic talking toilet bowl. Perfect, we thought, for little Noel Edmonds and the shambling Saturday morning hit show, *Multi-Coloured Swap Shop*.

Tim and I were duly invited to Television Centre to be assessed (I now realize) and to watch the programme from the gallery as it was transmitted. We seemed to pass some sort of BBC test because we were later booked to appear live on the 100th edition of *Swap Shop* which took place on the 1st November 1980 in the spacious surroundings of (the now demolished studio) TC7. Tim, (who had dragged along, for reasons still unclear, a young lady named Fiona Menzies), and I arrived at TVC at the appointed hour (9am) armed with our various bits of artwork. I had prepared these previously, several large, and not very accomplished, display strips concerning the programme. For example, the camera crew 13 was a running joke, plus a 'competition' cartoon and some prizes. We had no rehearsal as such, but were just shoved straight in to get on with it. The rigours of live TV.

Tim arguing the toss with Noel

Positioning ourselves at a table in the 'Coffee Shop', we awaited the time to be introduced. On cue, Noel immediately launched into a question about 'the dire state of comics today'. Tim then started to argue the point and I had to interject by declaring that what we were trying to do was 'very different', and then asking for a bigger table to draw my pictures on. Not a very good start. Things improved and during our next 'spot' and we managed to mention Marvel's *Future Tense* magazine five times in five minutes.

The morning raced by and all too soon it was over. We had met some nice people like the beautiful Jan Leeming, Maggie Philbin (equally beautiful) and Seb Coe, for whom I drew an instant caricature (I was warned in advance by one of the young ladies in his entourage that he was a bit sensitive about his nose). Seb had brought along his 1980 Moscow Olympics gold medal. I don't know what I was expecting to see, but the said medal looked to me suspiciously like a large gold foil covered chocolate penny.

Also on the show was dear old Matthew Waterhouse, the much pilloried actor who was then portraying the character Adric in *Doctor Who*. Like star-struck, disingenuous groupies we praised fulsomely Matthew for his recent performance as the latest *Who* companion number whatever...

Swap Shop regularly ran competitions and Tim and I had, as a prize a frameable colour cartoon, specially drawn by me. Also, we had other 'prizes', of which one of mine was a 1950 copy of the BBC Handbook. Gee, how interesting *that* must have been for the average pre-teen viewer! After the show, I got into conversation with the programme's editor, Rosemary Gill. She was leafing through my 1950 BBC Handbook 'prize' and alighted on a picture of very well-known female artiste. 'I could tell you some stories about her', said Rosemary. I was all ears but unfortunately Rosemary was interrupted at that juncture and I never got the dirt dished. All this social history just vanishing away. Poo! I don't know whether the BBC Archive has a recording of this 100th *Swap Shop* show. Probably, but I certainly do (on VHS). I would be willing to part with it, if requested, for a suitably large finder's fee.

Previous to our appearance on *Swap Shop*, Tim had alerted the editor of *Oh Boy* magazine, a ditzy publication for negligible intellects. The editor liked Tim's idea for a modern strip cartoon called *Livin' In The Eighties*. I then drew several pages of this stuff which was duly presented. However, the magazine's art director was totally unimpressed, criticizing my drawings as all having 'pointed noses' But the art director was overruled editorially, and off we went. From that juncture my published strips got smaller and smaller on the page until the only comfortable way to view them was with a portable electron microscope. Obviously, a nasty case of Art Director's Revenge. The strip was canned after ten myopic weeks.

Throughout the 1980s and the early 1990s our most enduring creation for Marvel was the *Doctor Who?* three-frame strip appearing in *Doctor Who Magazine*. This cartoon feature thrived under the changing editorships of notably Alan McKenzie, John Freeman, Gary Russell and Sheila Cranna. It helped very much that these editors had an abiding love for the *Doctor Who* programme and indeed, understood our take on the subject. It's generally acknowledged that our particular satirical cartoon slant on *Doctor Who* has never been equalled, spawning as it did many page features (*The Doctor Who History Tour*, *etc*.) and full colour strips in the various *Doctor Who* annuals. And then there was *The Doctor Who Fun Book* and *It's Bigger on the Inside*, both full of original strips and features. Lately, there has been the sell-out edition (and reprints) from MiWk Publishing entitled *It's Even Bigger on the Inside* which pulls together just about every Quinn and Howett *Doctor Who?* cartoon published, plus lots of private commissions never before seen in print, or indeed remembered by yours truly. However, now I think of it, I wonder what ever happened to the nude Peri cartoon I once sketched in a tipsy moment for a fan? The hunt is on!

And so on the basis of our *Doctor Who* magazine cartoon work, Tim and I spent the late 1980s traipsing the Fan Convention trail. Some big, some small. Actually I quite enjoyed these conventions as it raised the opportunity to meet fans and also hob nob with the stars of the programme. Nice meeting Sophie Aldred, Louise Jameson and Debbie Watling. Also glamour film actress Caroline Monroe, whom I'd last spotted semi-clad in an edition of *Men Only* magazine. Not certain why naughty Caroline was at the convention. She may have been a fan or perhaps seeking to be a companion? Larger on the scale of convention guests was Colin Baker and the slightly smaller Sylvester McCoy. Our *Doctor Who*

Fun Book had just been published and as a charity prize I asked the stars to sign a copy, although McCoy was rather grumpy about it. During these conventions, usually both Tim and myself sat at a corner desk where I drew little *Who* sketches (free of charge) and Tim practiced his signature. Later, Tim devised scripted performances whereby we both made fools of ourselves by reading, on stage, short 'joke' episodes of *Doctor Who*. There exists, I believe, a video of one our 'acts'. This will doubtless return to haunt us. Indeed, on one notable occasion, at a London Comics Convention, we were actually booed off stage by various fan boy drunks. At least they didn't throw anything.

Debbie Watling and me cuddling in a kitchen?

Radio and the Write Stuff

In 1986, BBC Essex, a new local radio station, began transmitting from studios in Chelmsford. I sauntered in with an idea for a series of *Tall Tales (of Essex)*, designed as a monthly slice of topical nonsense, read on-air by myself. I proposed taking a local news item (a new shopping centre, a new sports pavilion, road repairs or lack of them *etc.*) and then weaving an unlikely 'history' (this well before the advent of Fake News) all within the space of five minutes. A sort of aural cartoon strip. I wasn't a totally unknown entity to the corporation as at the time I was also the back-page cartoonist for the BBC's very own house journal *Ariel*, usually referred to by the wits at TV Centre as 'Pravda'. Incidentally, I had to be careful there. A cartoon of mine was praised for assisting in winning some sort of publishing prize for *Ariel*, but another cartoon I drew was dropped. This illustrated a piece about the recently established BBC Worldwide sales outfit. The cartoon depicted a spiv selling dodgy programmes captioned 'BBC WORLD *WIDE-BOY*'. Perhaps the editors didn't understand what a 'wide-boy' was... or indeed, dodgy programmes?

My *Tall Tales* scripts were written to incorporate music snatches interweaved as counterpoints (*The Sun Has Got His Hat On*, a few bars to indicate seasonally bad summer weather perhaps?). The first of my pre-recorded monthly *Tales* went out on Christmas Day 1986 and the second *Tale* went out on Boxing Day 1986, so from then on I was getting all behind.

I billed myself as the BBC Essex Alternative Historian, and although most of the listeners seemed unperturbed, or perhaps unaware, of my efforts to amuse, BBC Essex presenter Jules Bellerby absolutely hated my *Tall Tales*. Jules hosted the afternoon show and was obliged to run my offerings, usually without comment but occasionally with a snide aside. But I wasn't bothered, and in any case, a local publisher had bought a selection of my *Tall Tales* and had produced a nice little book, (still available on Amazon/eBay for a few pence) complete with my cartoon illustrations. When my book was launched, I was invited back onto

Jules' show to unmercifully publicize it. Well I never.

Telling Tall Tales in a bloody cold BBC studio (as usual).

But times they were a-changing. The Fleet Street revolution, spearheaded by the Murdoch press and anti-union legislation, facilitated mighty moves towards complete computerization of the national press and magazines. One corollary was that page make-up with scissors and a pot of paste was now performed exclusively on a computer screen, so there was no need for 'spot' cartoons to fill awkward spaces in the pagination. Gradually, I was selling fewer 'singles' and many of my steady markets vanished, seemingly overnight. As mentioned earlier, I decided to reboot my writing and photography skills by aiming illustrated (photos and cartoons) articles at specific niche publications. My interests were radio, TV, cinema and audio so I planned a variety of features around those themes. One described my adventures with Compact Discs, (quite new back then) another about the local Air Cadets video club and still another about my attempts to 'home movie' recalcitrant pets, all under the guise of *How To Flippin' Well Do It*. I even, for a while, had my own back page 'last word' feature called

Back Tracks in *Complete CD & Hi Fi Buyer* magazine. There I was, spinning the usual tall tales and plugging the merits of digital recording systems for the audiophiles. It's easy when you know absolutely nothing about the subject.

For my media articles I was constantly searching for suitable material. I then discovered a quaint, privately-financed magazine called *405-Alive* (run as a hobby), by technical journalist Andrew Emmerson. Andy's magazine was a delicious mixture of old time TV and folk memories, harking back to the good old days of black and white television. I contributed to Andy's magazine with an increasing amount of written material, concentrating on interviews with television luminaries, including directors, video technicians and premier TV technology manufacturers such as Marconi's, EMI or Vintens.

I found great delight in meeting and talking to these television old-timers. One such was Daphne Shadwell, a name perhaps unfamiliar to most, but Daphne directed the original 1960s ITV series of the frenetic TV pop music programme, *Ready Steady Go!*. She recalls, 'The title of the show actually came from me. Most TV directors started their programmes by counting down, "ten, nine, eight..." *etc.* I was different. I used to end the countdown with "ready, steady, GO!" That's how the show got its name. It was an in-joke'. Joke or not, *Ready Steady Go!* was innovative. Back in the 1960s, the current art form known as 'the pop promo' was then only a vague video notion. Spotty rock bands or solo singers could only promote their latest single live before unsympathetic cameras on 'square' programmes such as *Crackerjack!*, *Blue Peter* or *The Billy Cotton Band Show*.

Occasionally, a pop group might get full colour exposure on Rank's quirky and often sarcastic cinema series *Look at Life*, or be asked to make brief films for a short-lived system that used coin operated movie jukeboxes which played songs and ran films, sometimes in sync.

Originally, Daphne Shadwell wasn't connected with *Ready Steady Go!*. As a staff director at the ITV programme contractor, Associated-Rediffusion she worked on anything that came up, mainly women's and children's shows. 'I directed the *Five O'clock Club* which had quite a high pop music content. Muriel Young fronted that show and she also hosted a radio programme for

Luxembourg called *The Green Room* which was a pop record show with kids dancing and generally enjoying themselves. And then Elkan Allan, who was head of A-R's Light Entertainment, reported he'd seen the Dick Clark US pop show *American Bandstand* and wanted a similar show here. We combined Muriel's show with the Dick Clark programme format and that became *Ready Steady Go!*' Daphne Shadwell was the youngest of four daughters of BBC Variety Orchestra conductor Charles Shadwell and began her life in broadcasting as a humble (they are always 'humble') BBC secretary. Says Daphne, 'That was in 1947 in the Near East and Latin American Service of the BBC which was situated at Aldenham House, Elstree. It wasn't the most exciting of jobs, but in those days we were grateful for anything. However, I constantly applied for other posts within the BBC. I finally went to 200 Oxford Street, where they produced *Forces Favourites*. That was fun. We used to watch the world go by from our office, the Peter Robinson building high above Oxford Street.

'We used also to go swimming in our lunch hours at the nearby Marshall Street baths. We were reprimanded, however, for hanging our costumes out to dry on the balcony. Not very BBC!'

During 1947 Daphne Shadwell met her husband, TV director John P. Hamilton and they were married in 1954. The long courtship was out of necessity; they couldn't afford to marry on BBC wages! At the time, John P. was a BBC RPA (Recorded Programmes Assistant). He travelled the country with programmes such as *Down Your Way* and *Top of the Form*. Later, he added live spot effects on *The Goon Show*.

Back at Broadcasting House, Daphne Shadwell still applied for any BBC job going. It was while working in the BBC Duty room that she first entered television. 'In 1950 I became assistant to a producer called Pamela Brown,' says Daphne. 'Pamela Brown also used to write children's books, usually during BBC time which made her feel guilty. Anyway, I was sent down to Lime Grove; no training, never even been inside a studio before. I sat there open-mouthed watching a live cartoon show with Kenneth Connor voicing, *Simon the Simple Sardine*. Fascinating. I did everything on the production side, which is a good way to learn. Later, I was assistant to David Boisseau who directed *Muffin the Mule* up at Studio A, Alexandra Palace. Studio A had a production gallery

70

that was entered by climbing a steep flight of open stairs. In the room directly below these stairs was the Emitron camera control equipment. I caused a sensation by climbing up the stairs wearing a very short skirt. From that moment I was a big hit with the engineers!' Daphne Shadwell was soon directing cameras and artists. She became adept at calling shots, adding to her experience. In 1954, during a stint at Lime Grove, she met a *Whirligig* production assistant called Lloyd Williams who was surreptitiously recruiting BBC staff for the new commercial television station, Associated-Rediffusion. Daphne became Lloyd Williams' personal assistant at A-R with the promise of becoming a TV director herself when A-R started in 1955. Later, Daphne directed the Monty Python progenitor, *Do Not Adjust Your Set*, and also *Rainbow*, *Magpie*, *Splash*, and *The Sooty Show*.

Ready Steady Go! was produced live each Friday evening ('The weekend starts here!') from Studio 9 at A-R's Television House in Kingsway, London. The studio itself was small, (sixty-four foot by forty foot), and wedged-shaped with the scene doors orientated at the Bush House end of Kingsway. Daphne Shadwell, 'We crammed in about one hundred and twenty kids. We actually had a ticket waiting list of six thousand! With four large cameras and lights and everything, you can imagine it was a tight squeeze. But that's what made it so exciting. It was quite chaotic, but Keith Fordyce who introduced the show held everything together. It would all have fallen apart without him.'

An unusual feature of *Ready Steady Go!* was that no attempt was made to hide, on-screen, the TV cameras which could be observed amidst all the frantic pushing and shoving as they were maneuvered across the studio floor. Daphne recalled, 'It didn't start that way, having cameras in shot. On one show in 1963 we had Jerry Lee Lewis who was a bit rude to me. He didn't arrive until the final rehearsal and when I went onto the floor to check on a few points he bellowed "Who is this woman?" We hadn't been introduced, you see. Come the live show, he was of course marvellous and during the finale he stood up and hammered away at his piano. All the cameras moved in, and to my horror I saw that in every monitor, a camera was visible. I couldn't get away from them. It was a nightmare. So we just let them roll, and from then on if a camera got in shot, it stayed in shot!'

The camerawork on *Ready Steady Go!* was of a very high standard. The four studio cameras used were heavy and unwieldy. They were mounted on mechanical wheeled iron pedestals, which meant that cameramen had to heave at least 600lbs of equipment around the congested studio floor. Also, because the playback was extremely loud, the cameramen couldn't always hear the screamed instructions from the gallery, so they were relied on to offer shots. Some cameramen, like Bill Metcalf (who later became a BBC producer) had a natural gift and were always there when required, with an image correctly framed and interestingly shot. Other cameramen, perhaps used to leisurely discussion programmes or drama were not so responsive. However the studio cameras regularly rammed the audience. Daphne said, 'We always got injuries. It was the pan handles mainly that caught people in the back and on one occasion, a relative of Elkan Allan, a particularly obnoxious kid, was deliberately rammed.'

Ready Steady Go! made stars of Donovan, Billy Fury, Gene Pitney and 19-year-old Cathy McGowan, who chucked in a ten pound a week secretarial job to work on the show. 'Lovely girl, easy going,' recalls Daphne, 'not a brain in her head though. And the young American artists were also very nice to work with, very polite. Gene Pitney always joked that we tried every sort of entrance for him; outside in the scene dock, down stairs, up stairs, perhaps next he would be suspended from the lights! The studio was quite limited and the sets, quite basic, a few rostrums. Once we had Sonny and Cher and Cher brought in a dress she was going to wear for the transmission. The engineers wanted to test-light it and got Cher to hold the dress up in front of a camera. We actually forgot about her and later we noticed, what seemed like hours later, on the monitor, poor old Cher still standing patiently with her dress. We'd forgotten all about her, but she didn't complain or moan. Very professional'.

Daphne Shadwell has fond memories of her time as a TV director and especially the show, *Ready Steady Go!*. 'RSG was jolly hard work. My favourite pop groups were The Hollies and the Troggs. I christened them "The Trollies", especially when we had a hole in the bookings. "See if the Trollies are available," I'd say. Some pop artists baffled me. I thought Jimi Hendrix most peculiar and one group, The Small Faces, held up rehearsals once when the lead singer unaccountably disappeared for a whole afternoon. It turned out he'd been at Wembley hospital getting a fix! I never thought of such things like pot or drugs, although they were around. I was so innocent, but it explained Jimi Hendrix. I suppose people thought I was a bit quaint, especially when I used to hand out lollipop sweets to the crew at the end of transmission.'

Another interview was with TV director, Michael Leeston-Smith. He was a pioneer of post-war BBC television production who worked on the first two *Quatermass* series and also directed a *Doctor Who* story: *The Myth Makers*, so this was of particular interest to me.

Michael Leeston-Smith was employed first in 1932 at Ealing Studios as an assistant sound recordist on some of the Gracie Fields films. After war service, Leeston-Smith worked for the BBC at Alexandra Palace, initially on the transmitter and subsequently as a junior studio lighting engineer working with renowned director Rudolph Cartier on *The Quatermass Experiment*.

This seminal 'horror' production was performed live from Studio A. The working area was only about fifty foot by twenty-eight foot and the insensitive pre-war Emitron cameras demanded vast amounts of light, putting great demands on the actors who suffered terribly with the heat (this being mid-summer). Because of the Emitron camera's shading problems (stray electrons within the tube which caused the picture to look patchy) a regular cry heard from the production gallery was 'chicken on camera', referring to the shape of the fault. Leeston-Smith would then have to wheel five kilowatt spotlights to within a few feet of the actors in an attempt to iron out the 'chicken' and balance the picture. Sometimes things got so bad it was not unknown for the lighting level to be raised to ten kilowatt per actor!

Quatermass II (1955) was produced within the slightly more commodious surroundings of Studio G at Lime Grove. Working now as a production assistant, Leeston-Smith would accompany Rudolph Cartier on location filming. Leeston-Smith recalls, "We were filming at Shell Haven refinery. The morning had gone well with lots of film in the can. All taken in full sunlight. Then the clouds blotted out the light and we stopped until it cleared. We positioned the camera to film a shot of Quatermass in a car entering the main gate of the refinery. Just as the sun came out Rudi called "stand by, turn them over!" Suddenly the siren at Shell Haven, went off and crowds of staff came wandering out. It was lunch time and they all sat in the sunshine around the main gate eating sandwiches. Rudi cried, at me "Mike get rid of them. Why did you let this happen? What's the use of an assistant who lets things like this occur?" Then the sun went in for good.'

In 1961, after six years on the technical side, Michael Leeston-Smith was given the job of director. The Head of Drama at the time was Michael Barry who gave Leeston-Smith his chance, leading to directing many live episodes of the classic 1960s drama series *Z-Cars*. Leeston-Smith directed only one episode of *Doctor Who*. This was billed in the Radio Times as *Dr Who and the Trojan War*. 'John Wiles was a good producer,' says Leeston-Smith 'and it was great fun working with Max Adrian who played King Priam of Troy. Also Barrie Ingham who played Paris. Both marvellous actors.'

Although mainly studio-bound, this particular *Doctor Who* story demanded some outside filming, down at the often-used BBC location of Frensham Ponds. The BBC design department had constructed the necessary sets and the rest of 'Troy' was a model photographed using the 'Schufftan' process, a system devised by a German called Eugen Shufftan which involved an angled mirror with a section of the mirror's silver backing scraped off, then filming the reflected model combined with the live action beyond the hole. The wooden Trojan Horse was also a model and filmed similarly.

For a *Doctor Who Magazine* article, I tracked down a rather disgruntled retired BBC engineer called Joe Starie (described by colleagues as a 'legend in his own mind'). Joe worked at the BBC's Television Centre and in August 1963 was shift engineer when TC4 was booked for what was described as an 'experimental' session. The noted BBC designer Bernard Lodge was searching for a special effect in order to create a title sequence for a new drama production called *Doctor Who*. It was decided to try something called 'positive feed-back' or howl round. This effect is caused when electronic cameras 'see' their own output reflected back in a monitor and the image is repeated endlessly in a closed loop. These days that sort of effect can be digitally conjured, but back then it all had to be done optically and physically in the studio.

74

Joe Starie was called in and asked to set the position of an EMI 203 image orthicon camera and monitor. Says Joe, 'I began the electronic effect by keying the camera onto my pen-torch which I happened to have in my pocket. I waved the torch about for a few seconds and checked the monitor to see the results. The images started to show positive feedback. From then on I threw in everything I could offer. The most significant effects came when we reversed the scans in the camera which gave the now familiar swirling and twisting effect.'

The session lasted an hour and was recorded onto the old style 2-inch Quad videotape. Later, the best effects were chosen by the designer and mixed in with some previously filmed 'Doctor Who' title lettering. During our interview, Joe confessed that he had saved absolutely nothing from his days with the BBC, just his precious *Doctor Who* pen-torch that in retrospect, could have been said to have actually started it all.

Two Celebrity Twits on TV

Although I was now drawing and selling to fewer publications, one area that showed no signs of abating was the cartoon material I supplied to the men's top-shelf magazines. These included *Men Only*, *Penthouse*, *Mayfair*, *Razzle*, *Girl Illustrated* (yes, the magazine featuring a tumescent Dalek and a nude *Doctor Who* companion, the lovely Katy Manning), *Fiesta*, *Knave*, *Escort*, *The Journal Of Sex* (I wonder what that was all about) and Paul Raymond's *Club International*. I had a colour three-frame strip running in *Club International* called *Movie Millie*. Millie, bless her heart, was a, 'adult' star who, was teamed with Big John, a prodigious chap who could 'extend' himself at least forty-five feet. Big John once had a cold and came to the studio with a very long, suspiciously red sausage-shaped 'scarf' wrapped around his neck many times. What fun we had.

A Movie Millie somewhat cleaner than usual

I found that the editors for these adult magazines were by far the easiest to deal with. They seemed almost pathetically grateful for my cartoon work, but then I suppose there weren't many of us willing, or indeed able to draw the naughty stuff. Anyway, the pay rates were far above Fleet Street and so I just continued to churn it out and rake in the lolly. Years later in 2012, I was filming with Steve Coogan on *The Look of Love*, a Channel 4 biopic, based on the life of Paul Raymond. The location that day was in Berwick Street, Soho and opposite the pokey little *Club International* office where I used to deliver my *Movie Millie* cartoons.

Singular commissions sometimes arose. I was contracted to draw a daily three-frame cartoon strip for a Zambian newspaper. Now, to be honest, I was a little doubtful. A year or so previously, Tim and I had drawn a comic page for a Nigerian magazine which never paid us. The Zambian commission was different inasmuch that it was funded from a UK agency and the money was paid in advance. All I had to do was draw the life history of Zambia's president, Mr Kenneth Kaunda. Well why not, I reasoned? The fact that the fee was quite large helped to dispel any further doubts.

The script was written by a freelance writer whose name escapes me, but the slight difference here for me was that the strip wasn't in any way to be humorous, just a straight forward illustrated history of a real person. The apparent reason for the strip was that Kenneth Kaunda was standing for re-election and it was thought that a nice illustrated hagiography would help his chances. This seemed to me, unlikely. But as Tesco might say, every little helps.

I didn't follow subsequent events in Zambia so I've no idea of the eventual outcome of the election, but I was informed that although the commissioners liked my strip cartoon, which I drew in advance amounting to forty two daily instalments, it was never actually published. Seemed a waste of the £1,800 they paid me. But thanks indeed for that all the same. I had fulfilled what I had been asked to do.

Back in the UK, in 1985 the Dundee publishers, D.C. Thompson had a prescient idea. Initially dubbed 'Project AM' it eventually emerged as *Celebrity* magazine, and it did exactly as described on the tin. The magazine was a precursor to all the *Hello*s, *Heat*s, *OK*s and *Goodbye*s *etc.* that were later to grace the 'celebrity' publishing scene.

Tim and I submitted a strip called *G.E.T.* (apparently, a mild Liverpudlian insult) or *Great Enormous Twit*. This *G.E.T.* was a tale of other worlds and space ships with the eponymous hero Kevin Block zipping around the galaxy having spiffing adventures. DCT replied, (I have all the letters and extracts follow). *'Many thanks for submitting your G.E.T. space cartoons... also we envisage changing the title to Twit in Space which actually fits quite well with your own translation of Great Enormous Twit.'* So Tim didn't get (as it were) away with *that* one!

*Twit In Space original artwork. Generally the colour
reproduction in Celebrity magazine was crap.*

The *Twit* commission proceeded and I completed colour art
work having first submitted pencil roughs prepared from Tim's
scripts. These roughs were very important to the editors as it gave
them ample opportunity to actually do a spot of editing. For
example, editorial advice about Rough number 16: *'It concerns the
"spitting" incidents, sorry not very Thomson-like. Not even
"tasteful" spitting!'* or *'...not too keen on your "subliminal
advertising ending"'* or *'...we once had a bit of bother with the
Blue Peter producer so I'd appreciate it if you could water down
that association in episode 27.'*

Intriguing. However, occasionally my roughs were returned
having been tampered with, bits of dialogue or images altered, and
commented upon thus *'...thanks for roughs... episodes 40 to 45,
no problems here apart from No. 42 which we'd like to drop.'* No
explanations were forthcoming here about any perceived problems
with rough No. 42 but recently I found this rough and it's one
of my favourites. It shows Kevin and Rabbie the Robot crashing
through four cartoon 'frames', Plop! Plop! Plop! Plop! with a tag
line about an emergency stop button. I cannot fathom the

objection to this very nice (if I say so myself) bit of drawing and clever scripting. It actually encapsulated the Quinn and Howett cartoon humour approach and *raison d'etre*. Ho hum.

Perhaps they didn't fancy the word 'plop'

Eventually *Twit in Space* ended with issue 46 and it was replaced with some vapid humorous cartoon concoction more in keeping with editorial remits. Re-reading my correspondence with the editors of *Celebrity* magazine, I now get the distinct impression that they never *really* understood the humour of *Twit in Space*. I think, they just encouraged us as a kindness. So as a *Twit* character, Rabbie the Robot might have said, 'They may have laughed at Thomas Edison, but no' at the Glasgee Empire they didnae.' Nor apparently, at dear old Dundee DCT.

Tim's next spiffing wheeze was to reform and reinvent us both as television 'film critics'. Thus was born *Tim and Dicky's Take Two*. During Tim's sojourn in the United States (working for the *Saturday Evening Post Magazine*) he had come across a syndicated TV show hosted by a couple of film critics called Gene Siskel and

Roger Ebert. Apparently this programme was extremely popular featuring as it did two eminent journalists, both with an encyclopaedic knowledge of Cinema. Tim had envisioned us doing likewise on British TV, disregarding the fact that we weren't in any way eminent journalists nor did we have the least part of an encyclopaedic knowledge of Cinema.

Tim arranged a meeting with the producers. This was for an ITV programme called *This Morning*, broadcast daily by Granada Television from the historic, and recently restored, Albert Dock complex in Liverpool. The thrust of our TV idea was in the form of a two handed criticism of current movies, with a 'one for' and 'one against' approach, giving 'thumbs up or down' to any given film. The idea seemed okay to me, if a little contrived. The nub of this exercise was the interaction between us as 'critics' and the resulting 'entertainment value' so derived. Thus *Tim and Dicky's Take Two* aired on the 21st February 1989. It really should have been *Take One* because that was the first and last time it was ever seen.

What we did was this. We had two current movies lined up to 'criticize'. *Gorillas in the Mist* and *Fatal Attraction* (out on video in 1989). I professed to 'like' *Gorillas* and 'hate' *Fatal*. Tim, the opposite reaction. Previously we had obtained VHS copies of these films in order to review the subject matter and concoct our comments. *This Morning* then obtained broadcast quality extracts to transmit. We arrived at the studio, in good time for our rehearsal, and to cue up the film extracts. We had scripted everything and timed our performance to around eight minutes. Annoyingly, we never got our rehearsal, as something else intervened which needed the time. So, there we were, about to go out live on national TV, with a fully unrehearsed segment, trying desperately to read everything off autocue, something, I personally had never done in my life, (not at all difficult as it turned out). The programme started (hosted by singer Paul Jones and his wife, who were booked as holiday replacements for the usual presenters, Punch and Judy).

Tim and I crept into our small 'cinema' set (popcorn, red plush seats, cigarette smoke- a studio assistant was behind us on the floor puffing a cigar for the effect) and awaited our cue to begin. During an ad break a frantic floor manager rushed over and asked us to cut our eight minutes down to five 'as we are overrunning!' We staggered through as best we could and finished more or less within the niggardly time allowed. Not our finest hour, I fear, nor indeed five minutes. We made the best of it, but I had a premonition that we were not really cut out to be TV stars and we would only have crash landed and been at odds with management at some point. Reviewing later the VHS off-air copy of our appearance, I noticed a sign hanging from the curtain behind us with read in large letters, 'Gentlemen's Cloakroom'. It seemed like a very unfair criticism of our masterly performances, down the pan again.

Sign of the times

With another prospective TV career aborted we both, more in desperation I fear, had a try at the 'alternative' comics then in vogue (*Smut*, *Acne*, *Fizz*, *etc.*), but I personally had no enthusiasm for this sort of arch 'amateur' publication. We placed a few strips including *Bloody Ages Ago* and *Doug & Del they Undertake Quite Well* (the less said about that the better!). To cap it all, our *Doctor Who?* strip had ground finally to a halt after around 224 editions, mainly because the *Doctor Who Magazine* publishers had sold the title to Panini and I suppose they wanted a different 'look'. So there it ended. Question: Were we running out of ideas? No. Question: Were we too expensive? Not really. The outcome, all change   for the sake of it. And why not? Give somebody else a crack at it. Humour as we all know is easy, anyone can do it. However, let me state right here and now that there has never been a feature quite like our *Doctor Who?* This is a boast I can expect, with confidence, to go completely and utterly unchallenged.

The Higher We Go...

My cartooning collaborations with Mr Quinn had apparently now ceased and desisted, so he and I both went our merry ways. I was still obtaining cartooning commissions. I produced a small range of greetings cards, even seaside postcards. Another was for a delightful series of 'humour' books produced by Brockhampton Press, entitled *The Funny Book Of...* They were handy, 60-page pocket-sized, inexpensive publications, the sort you see on souvenir stall spinner racks. I contributed colour cartoons for the books, interspersed between the text 'jokes' which were selected by Karen Sullivan and Bob Hale. I was given very much a free hand and submitted roughs for selection. My cartoon subjects were 'Golf', 'Mothers In Law', 'Fathers' and 'After Dinner Stories'. I managed to infiltrate a *Doctor Who* gag with an 'after dinner speaker' Dalek giving a 'Knock Knock, Who's There' speech. Oh the wit of it all.

Back at Fleet Street, Gerald Lip, cartoon editor of the *Daily Star* ('*Star Fun*') was still buying my 'spot' cartoons. (*The Sun* and the *Daily Mirror* were now about the only other national press with a cartoon page. The *Mirror* also ran a short-lived feature cartoon series, to which I contributed, called *Funny Money*. No reflection on the fee, naturally).

Gerald Lip was a very nice guy and also a cartoonist himself. However, Gerald got himself into a spot of bother. During the mid-1990s a newspaper 'war' erupted. A new London evening paper was produced and rival publishers attempted a 'spoiler'. They revived the old long-defunct *London Evening News* which was full of not much except quite a few of my 'spot' cartoons. Gerald had asked me for anything 'London' themed, so I quickly submitted a batch of cartoons, most of which were printed in a single edition! Thus on one glorious *day* I earned £250! This enraged other cartoonists who incorrectly assumed that I had the sole rights to submit material. This eventually sorted itself and quite soon the 'new' old spoiler *London Evening News* vanished along with my nice little daily earner.

Early in 1997, Letts Educational publications contacted me.

Would I please illustrate a series of 'primers'? Of course. No sweat. The fee was an astounding £3,000. I began work at once producing full colour roughs of an apposite and humorous nature. Previously, I'd illustrated the *Which Guide To Hi Fi* and so I ploughed on in a similar vein in my usual inimitable and carefree way. Big shock. My commission was cancelled suddenly. Apparently the editorial team had decided, belatedly, on a single 'cute' character (a Smurf lookalike) with no 'humour' attached. This was being drawn by a piss poor in-house artist. So all that creative work down the drain. Thanks a lot! I eventually settled for 50% of the fee, but that was not the point. I had really looked forward to this commission and now it had been scuppered by some berk of an editor. So there and then I gave it all up. It was the year 1997 and I resolved *never* again to draw a cartoon for a paying publication.

I Go Clubbing

My perambulations within the world of magazine feature-scribing lead me inexorably to The British Amateur Television Club which as the name suggests is a club for British amateur television clubbers. Historically, it was during 1949 that the BATC (as abbreviated) was formed in order to promote 'Ham Television'. This was where electronics enthusiasts built their own licensed 'shack' TV stations (usually literally in a shack) and viewed each other (*hello G8 XYZ*) on restricted transmission bandwidths (usually 70cms). One restriction was that nothing smacking of 'entertainment value' was allowed to be broadcast. Witnessing recently these 'ham' transmissions, the TV clubbers are certainly still adhering to *that* golden rule.

I obtained a commission from a magazine called *Production Solutions* to cover the annual BATC Rally which was a vast boot fair and exhibition, an outing for members and families. In 1998 it was held at the Sports ConneXtion, near Coventry. I interviewed various people and took a few snaps for editorial use. Mostly, the conventioneers were intent of selling redundant equipment but others were on the hunt for memorabilia. One interviewee was John van Dyke a freelance floor manager – ex-BBC – who was looking for anything connected with *The Black and White Minstrel Show*, books or tapes (the BBC have hardly any recordings of this programme, nor likely ever to show them again.) John had been floor manager for some of the early Minstrel colour recordings at BBC Television Centre and indeed married one of the dancers, so he had a specific interest.

Another interested party was Andy Emmerson. As mentioned earlier, Andy edited a nostalgia-driven, pre-colour TV magazine called *405-Alive*. I reported Andy as saying, 'These days it's only at electronics rallies like this that you can find old PYE monitors or perhaps back copies of ITV Yearbooks. That sort of nostalgia is getting hard to find and dealers are charging prices to match'. Indeed, current prices on eBay for 1960s copies of those ITV Year Books can now exceed £100. Also, at one of these BATC Rallies, I had met electronics engineer Paul Marshall and by doing

85

so, this chance meeting opened up an entirely new career for me, of which more later.

By now, I was a perceived as a 'Television History Expert'. Be that as it may, I had a least worked in the medium and had now begun to collect items of historic TV studio technical equipment. With these modest recommendations draped about me, I was invited to become, and as far as I can tell, still am, a member of an outfit called The Alexandra Palace Television Trust (not to be confused with the Alexandra Palace Trust or The Alexandra Palace Television Society). The Television Trust's sole aim was to preserve for posterity the fabric of the two areas within Alexandra Palace which formed the original 1936 BBC television studios. This television trust was an adjunct to the main AP Trust. Both trusts functioned under the auspices of Haringey Council. It didn't help that both trusts were constantly besieged by a gaggle of self-interested 'developers', obstructionists and monumental egotists. Also, it didn't further the Television Trust's *raison d'etre* when a few of its own trustees were constantly at logger heads with each other and everybody else for that matter.

We bumbled along with tiresome monthly meetings, held sometimes at Alexandra Palace itself, but usually we had to meet a few miles away at an old converted former public convenience inhabited currently then by the Hornsey Historical Society. One of my first suggestions as a Trustee, (and which was acted upon), was to shift all the 'exhibition' equipment (of which there was a confusing and dilapidated collection) from the ground floor up to one of the studios. This made sense to me as it was a better venue to attract possible funds for our projected conducted tours. The studios themselves were in a neglected state. There were multiple holes in the roof, attendant scuttling vermin, pigeon poo and rickety flooring, the usual result of British indifference to its heritage.

To set a context, it was in 1935 that the BBC chose a crumbling Victorian edifice in North London named Alexandra Palace to house its proposed new-fangled television service. Alexandra Palace was, at that time, a commercial white elephant containing several dilapidated exhibition areas, a theatre and a couple of interconnecting banqueting halls. These two halls, each thirty foot by seventy foot, were transformed into prototype television studios with electronic control areas, fitted adjacent. On one of the four

86

corners of the building, a transmitter tower, (still there), was positioned. This took advantage of the three hundred foot location height of Alexandra Palace which was ideal for the VHF transmitter beam. This had a 'line of sight' range of approximately thirty miles. In 1936, this was sufficient to cover a quarter of the population of the UK.

In mid-1936 BBC Television began operations (programmes beamed to Radiolympia) but it soon became apparent that the Alexandra Palace studios were cramped and inconvenient. Added to which, the studios were situated on the first floor and so all the scenery, props and electronics had to be winched from ground level. Nevertheless, television prospered, and apart from a break during the second world war, the Alexandra Palace studios produced several memorable live programmes, not least of which was, in 1953, *The Quatermass Experiment*.

The Television Trust and I struggled on grimly, amidst petty shenanigans and needless point scoring. One of the aims of this Trust, or so I imagined, was to preserve and perhaps reinstate the old studios as an educational resource. To this end, an ill-conceived feasibility study, paid for by an Arts Council grant, was commissioned from a company of surveyors. Their eventual conclusion, after much delay, proved that creating an exhibition and projected four-wall studio hire area within the existing space was unfeasible. As somebody who had worked in TV, I was a little nonplussed that the survey company hadn't asked me one single question or even asked for advice. Many other fanciful schemes for the studios came and went, including demolition entirely.

In 1996, the shambolic Television Trust just about managed to organize a 60th birthday party for the TV Studios and we invited several notables including the former BBC television announcer, Sylvia Peters, who cut the celebratory cake and spoke a few well-chosen words. After, she allowed me to kiss her cheek which was very much a plus of the evening. All progressed reasonably smoothly, but I learned subsequently of an undercurrent of much ill-temper and bitchiness from certain Trust members. After much hand wringing and teeth sucking, I decided I'd had enough and called it a day. Trust me, I'm a Television Trustee. No thanks.

An original 1937 Emitron tv camera, the type used by the BBC well into the 1950s. The camera had an interlaced scan rate of 405-lines and photographed in black and white using a single 6"inch f3.5 lens. The camera needed plenty of light to give a good picture. It seemed to work most of the time. Very few off-screen recordings exist taken with this type of camera.

Later in 2011, a smaller scale celebration, this time the 75th anniversary was held, again, in Studio A. For this, the Bradford-based National Media Museum kindly loaned, from their collection, one of the original BBC Emitron studio cameras. Only a very few of this camera type were ever manufactured and only a handful, in various states of integrity, remain. I'm constantly surprised how *small* the Emitron camera was, until I remembered that most of the camera's control apparatus (the size of two large bedroom wardrobes) was tucked away in the bowels of Camera Control. The Museum's camera looked brand new, evidence that it had been well looked after (or perhaps extensively restored, because it certainly didn't look as if it had been subjected to the usual BBC TLC). During the party, and feeling a bit reckless, I managed to prise off the camera's top. Unfortunately, the Emitron's Iconoscope imaging tube was missing. Apparently, it was too fragile to risk installing for the exhibition. Understandable, when one considers that these tubes are quite rare and irreplaceable.

Previously, I mentioned that my meeting with engineer Paul Marshall had proved fortuitous. Paul, an ex-Marconi employee, collected old, redundant and heavyweight television cameras, especially ones manufactured by the Marconi Company. It was a crazy hobby as Paul would be the first to admit. All this early TV technology was, and is, weighty and space consuming. However, Paul had a particular interest which involved restoration and preservation coupled with his acknowledged talent for electronics. Earlier, Paul had stored all his cameras and electronic bric-a-brac in his bachelor accommodation which was part of a three storey town-house in Sunrise Avenue, Chelmsford. This intrigued me because I too had lived in a three storey town house in Sunrise Avenue, Chelmsford. In fact Paul had lived in the *very same house*. It transpired that Paul had sub-let from a colleague, another Marconi engineer, who had bought the house from us when, in 1979, we had moved to a larger property a few miles away.

My conversation with Paul occurred at a BATC rally where Paul was exhibiting a few of his classic Marconi TV cameras. Naturally, I wanted some of *those!* I began at once to hunt for redundant TV camera equipment, a search which lead me to a local Chelmsford scrap heap and thence to an entirely new career, a career later involving me in award-winning television drama, Hollywood blockbuster movies and several exhibitions in the Royal palaces of England.

Reeling back to 1956 and that ATV Southend-on-Sea outside broadcast, with my younger self posing beside a real live TV camera, forty years later, I aimed to buy such a camera. Not easy, in fact, seemingly impossible. Most broadcast television camera equipment was manufactured in relatively small quantities and had a finite life span of ten years or so. After that period, TV companies scrapped or recycled the stuff. The BBC had its own redundant equipment store at Avenue House, Power Road, Chiswick. Sometimes the lucky recipients of these time-expired cameras were foreign 'emerging' broadcasters, or possibly educational establishments with nascent media courses. Once, I tracked down a likely camera but it was reposing, inconveniently, in a shed in Ethiopia!

My first old TV purchase was a pair of 1960s camera headphones. It was a start. But I was determined to acquire the big stuff and between 1992 and 1995 I took possession of a succession of classic electronic items including an EMI 2001 colour camera (ex-Anglia TV) a Pye Mk 3 (ex-ATV – yes, the very same type as depicted in my Southend photo!) an EMI 203 camera from Lime Grove Studios and a mighty 1950s era Marconi Mk III camera from the BBC Manchester Dickenson Road studios. These Manchester studios had previously produced the delights of such as *Top Of The Pops*, *Val Doonican* and *Pinky and Perky* so I can claim with confidence that my camera had truly rubbed shoulders with the musical elite. But it was now 1996 and I decided that it was time to build an extension to my home.

Propping Up

During the 1990s I was steadily building my collection which now included ancillary items such as microphones, studio lighting, lenses and tripods. Even movie cameras. I'm asked usually, how I find this equipment. Basically it's word of mouth or recommendation. An early lead was from an acquaintance who mentioned perhaps that a camera or two might be buried under a pile of scrap at a Chelmsford metal reclaimers. This info didn't seem at all likely. However, on the off chance that this tip might prove correct, I visited the scrapyard and uncovered no less than *eight* ancient television cameras, all jumbled up and in various states of disrepair. These cameras, which dated from 1951, included two American models that had somehow drifted over from a Los Angeles TV station called KHJ-TV. Unbelievable. It transpired that all these cameras had been acquired originally by the Chelmsford company EEV as redundant stock to test drive their valves and image tubes.

It hadn't really occurred to me that my collection of television camera equipment could be used as props for movies or TV. But eventually this is precisely what happened. Those scrap cameras recovered from the Chelmsford junk yard, (and others), have since travelled the length of Europe appearing as authentic props in several movies, including a Dublin location (*Evelyn*) with Pierce Brosnan and another in Berlin (*Beyond The Sea*) with Kevin Spacey. Also, many home grown TV dramas including *The Hour* and the *Doctor Who* anniversary drama *An Adventure in Space and Time*. Crowning this, in 2013 a special 60th Coronation Anniversary exhibition was held during the Summer months at Buckingham Palace, and yes, yet again one of those scrapyard cameras was on display, looking every bit the pristine original 1953 Marconi machine. Even, would you believe, in June of 2013 as a BBC Camera exhibit in the foyer for the opening ceremony of the Corporation's billion quid 'New' Broadcasting House. And so it goes.

Previously, Paul Marshall and I had agreed to split the hiring of our TV equipment. This meant that our by now substantial collections constituted an enormous catalogue, (including several classic and rare movie cameras), rivalling anything available anywhere in the world. To date, this arrangement has worked well. We call ourselves *Golden Age TV*, it's all in the name, but still we get enquiries from untutored tyro production assistants seeking spiral staircases, old chimney pots or hurricane lamps.

Silly requests aside, for the past twenty nine years, Paul and I have provided a unique service, hiring items as small as a microphone up to a large outside broadcast truck. In 2005, we hit the big time when we shipped to Hungary, almost *four and a half tons* of vintage television and film equipment for a Universal Pictures movie project. Initially, this project was shrouded in secrecy with even sniffer dogs on set. Later it was revealed as being the Oscar nominated film *Munich*, the director, Steven Spielberg.

But why four and a half tons of movie props? It goes like this. Something called 'Show and Tell'. Mr Spielberg, as he was addressed, required a choice. We assembled and arranged all our shipped kit in an airfield hanger at one of the locations, and Mr Spielberg came in, saw the 'show' and told us what he wanted. Expensive when considering that only about a third of our equipment was chosen and even less was seen in the final cut. Nevertheless, it was very much a master class in megabucks Hollywood blockbusting.

For *Munich* we spent a happy September week in Budapest, but as most of our scenes were scripted for shooting at night, we slept during the day and awoke to have our breakfast at 5.30 in the afternoon. Unsettling. Some major scenes took place at an old Soviet-era airfield called Tokol. During one night of shooting, I supervised the handling our props and when I returned early in the morning to the Budapest hotel, my wife counted ninety mosquito bites on my back. Strangely, during the shoot, I was totally unaware of the little nippers.

I had decided now to concentrate exclusively on my prop-hiring business. Having already abandoned my cartooning career, I also abandoned media writing. To be honest, I had just about covered everything and markets were changing yet again.

In 2006, Kelly Publications printed my book, *Television*

Innovations: *50 Technological Developments*, which was a compendium of some of my many media articles, illustrated with photographs. It was a nice little production and the cover price was not too expensive, (available still as a free Kindle version). The book was intended as essentially, a non-technical media primer, produced to familiarize students with the history of television broadcast hardware and also for geeks who just liked drooling over images of old TV cameras. Whatever, sales were modest.

One of my heavier cameras with a lighter Sylvester McCoy

An early dip (February 1996) into the wonderful world of prop hire was via Keith Barnfather of Reeltime Pictures. Keith wanted me to supply two classic television cameras for one of his *Doctor Who* sell-through VHS tapes. This edition was called *I Was A Doctor Who Monster* and featured interviews with the poor sods who were routinely stuffed into a Dalek chassis or coated with colourful gunk in the name of TV terror. On this occasion, I co-opted my brother Stephen and between us we trundled the cameras, mics and pedestals to the former BBC Riverside Studios, near Hammersmith. We prepared several scenes recreating past *Doctor Who* episodes using lookalike actors and a sink plunger representing a Dalek. Ex-Doc Sylvester McCoy presided with Sophie Aldred in attendance. All went reasonably sweetly and we met some nice people including actor Peter Hawkins, whom I remember primarily as the voice of Mr Turnip and Porterhouse the Parrot.

My ever-expanding camera collection required yet another move, this time into the rural Essex countryside. I needed a house with grounds in order to spread. My 'hobby' was going places and so was I. We found a detached house in a modest village, and promptly demolished the old wooden garage, erecting in its place a thirty-five foot 'play room', at least that's what I called it on the planning application.

As a rule, wherever possible, I travel with my cameras to the various studios or locations. I do this to protect my precious things from careless handling. During shoots I assist and also I can usually inveigle the production into hiring me as an S.A. or Supporting Artist, even my wife Margaret achieved this during some studio scenes for a BBC 2 drama '*We're Doomed! The Making Of Dad's Army.*' They dressed her fetchingly as 'Script Lady'. For all this, additional fees are paid and also a possible and fleeting appearance in the finished product. To date I've been a pretend cameraman in over sixty productions, spanning the decades, from the 1940s to the 1990s. However, the casual viewer will note that I never seem to age. Only my hair style alters from long to short and back again plus wearing the same old deathless combination of brown tie, brown trousers and brown woolly jumper.

Thus, fully browned off, Golden Age TV has helped recreate scenes from many iconic television programmes including *Steptoe and Son, Coronation Street*, The 1953 Coronation BBC broadcast (three times), *Sunday Night At The London Palladium, What's My Line, The Brains Trust, Double Your Money, Thunderbirds, This Is Your Life, Top Of The Pops, Pot Black, The Sky At Night, Dad's Army, Crossroads,* and *Doctor Who*. Also television and movie dramas involving the lives of, in no particular order, Tommy Cooper, Cilla Black, Hughie Green, Tony Hancock, Fanny Cradock, Lord Lucan, John Stonehouse, Lord Longford, Bobby Darin, Diana Princess of Wales, (twice)

94

Mr Rogers (US) Margaret Thatcher, Hattie Jacques, Paul Raymond, Morecambe and Wise, Elizabeth Taylor, Richard Burton, Richard Nixon, John Lennon, Laurel and Hardy, (twice) Mary Whitehouse, Brian Clough, George Best, Christine Keeler, Enid Blyton, Alexander Korda, Hurricane Higgins, Peter Sellers, Kenny Everett, Franklin D Roosevelt, Sir Winston Churchill, Boy George, Eddie The Eagle, Noele Gordon, Sir Anthony Eden, Freddie Mercury, Rupert Murdock, Bob Marley, Leonard Bernstein, Bobby Moore, Paddington Bear and Sooty.

In 2009, I was hired, along with one of my old 35mm movie cameras, to recreate a scene with actress Helena Bonham Carter who was playing the part of Enid Blyton for a BBC 4 drama (back in the day when BBC 4 regularly commissioned such productions) called appropriately enough, *Enid*. I arrived at Longcross Studios (a former MOD tank factory and military test site near Chertsey) and installed my 1940s newsreel 35mm camera for a Blyton family scene. For this we used a 'dressed' lounge, one of the many rooms situated in a real mansion positioned in the grounds of the studios. (used currently for the interior and exterior scenes of Nonnatus House and Call the Midwife). I was bundled over to 'costume' and fitted with a period tweed (brown) suit and a natty moustache, ready to play my part as a 1943 'Pathe' newsreel camera chappie.

The scene was set, with the Blyton family playing a game of Snakes and Ladders. On 'Action!' the real movie camera focused on myself pretending to film Helena and the two child actors, all positioned in front of a roaring fire. As is the usual practice in films, the 'fire' is a combination of imitation fire-proof logs and a self-lighting gas burner that can easily be switched on and off between takes. At the final take the gas fire was extinguished. This held a fascination for one of the child actors who announced, 'That fire is fake!' to which Helena replied, 'We're *all* fake here, darling.'

My life of churning out cartoons for the penny dreadfuls was now well and truly over as my progress as prop supplier to the movie world became established. I recall also that the Winter of 2010/2011 was *very* cold. This was the period in which we filmed *The Hour*, a sorely underrated BBC 2 serial drama set in the world of BBC Television circa 1956. My task, along with my colleague Paul, was to fully equip a Lime Grove BBC television studio with correct period cameras, lights, microphones and picture monitors.

Earlier, the production designer for the series, Eve Stewart, had visited my house for a chat. Eve (*Les Miserables*, *The King's Speech*, *The Damned United*, *The Danish Girl*) was tasked with visualizing, not only the studio spaces, but also the production offices and cutting rooms. Eve needed advice and also some idea of the 1950s television technology used. I gave Eve a conducted tour of my collection, pointing out relevant items such as cameras, pedestals, microphone booms, lamps, and also the practicalities of 'pretending' to make fifty year-old equipment work. I explained to Eve that the trick is to implant modern electronics and imperceptibly hide it within the original shell or casing. With generally tight budgets, it's understood that TV productions can't afford to hang about if the old stuff packs up at the critical moment. A modern implant will run all day. Fit and forget. Smoke and Mirrors.

Golden Age TV was commissioned to supply all the television studio and film equipment for both series of *The Hour*. The series was made by the estimable production company, Kudos. Paul and I had never before undertaken such an extensive commission, but we rose to the occasion, installing three iconic Marconi television cameras, one perched on a mobile mechanical crane. I even wangled myself the job as Script Consultant, checking for technical anachronisms and inconsistencies. Also, Paul and I resumed our on-screen roles as 'studio cameramen', wearing the same old dun-coloured outfits! Incidentally, *The Hour* is (to date) the only BBC Television programme to give Golden Age TV an on-screen credit. Apparently humble props companies *never* get a BBC puff.

Eve Stewart's, eventual studio designs bore little resemblance to the 'real' Lime Grove, but that wasn't the point. The reconstructions had the feel of an old 1950s television studio, as well as being ergonomically built so that the Director of Photography could easily manoeuvre his high-definition, digital ARRI ALEXA camera, as and when required. *The Hour* starred Romola Garai, Dominic West, Ben Whishaw and the charming Anna Chancellor, who for some obscure reason, wanted to have her photograph taken with me. Must have been the heady attraction of my exotic brown woolly jumper!

*Anna Chancellor Ben Whishaw and me (doing my Wallace &
Gromit impression). Dom West in the background. Yes it
was cold at that location. Ben in thick coat and hot water
bottle. We had industrial heaters but they couldn't be
used during 'takes' because of the noise.*

Pause between 'Takes'

Ben as 'Freddie Lyon' awaits his cue on The Hour

And was it cold in November 2010? You bet, especially at Hornsey Town Hall. The old Town Hall, near Crouch End in London, was built in the early 1930s. In 1986 it had been closed and deemed redundant due to local authority mergers and changes. Since then the Town Hall had limped along as an arts centre and latterly as rental space for TV and movies. For The Hour production, some of the interior spaces and rooms of the old Town Hall were used for the office and studio sequences. The main large theatre space was reconstructed as Lime Grove Studio E. Adjoining offices were dressed as newsrooms, edits suites, and for Series Two, even a Soho night club. Unfortunately, for us, the main theatre space was completely unheated and so we shivered most of the time despite several industrial space heaters blasting away between takes. The glamour of movie-making, can't beat it.

We were a little disappointed later to learn that there was to be no series Three of The Hour. Over the previous months, we had built a good working relationship with the production company, staff and actors, and in particular the lead players. The programme was aired originally on BBC2 and BBC America, and although the first series' ratings were good, apparently they fell away during Series Two. The very last scene of Series Two had Ben Whishaw as Freddie Lyon laying stabbed and bloody on a grassy verge outside the studio doors. Did he die or did he recover? Unfortunately, we shall never know. Although the two series were later released on DVD, the series has, to date never been re-shown on mainstream tv.

Apart from making a few quid hiring my collection, a corollary is that I never know what will turn up next. Sometimes it's the same old video hire, using myself and one of my 'analogue' tube colour cameras to film the 'look' of a 1970s and 1980s pop show. But what came completely out of the blue was a commission from the famous London store, Selfridges. They wanted Golden Age TV to dress *eleven* Oxford Street windows with movie and video equipment. We were to supply cameras, tripods and lights. Our equipment was to complement various fashions provided by designers such as Stella McCartney, Paul Smith, Thom Brown, Yohji Yamamoto and Jean Paul Gaultier. Themed as 'The Masters', our cameras were positioned amongst the frocks and suits with oblique references to famous movies and directors. Not entirely successful perhaps, being somewhat esoteric, unless you were a film buff or a fan of expensive couture. Or both. Or neither....

For these multi-window dressings, our equipment had been shipped earlier to the Oxford Street store. Later, Paul and I assisted in assembling all the eleven windows. This had to be undertaken from 10pm when the store closed for the night. We were still there at 2am the following morning. Quite an experience, especially when three months later we repeated the entire process and repacked everything, again well into the wee small hours. Thus the Summer of 2014 was a proverbial showcase for our cameras. Coincidentally, I'd also tailored another window display (an Auricon 16mm movie camera) which featured in the Old Bond Street upmarket clothing store DAKS. All told, 2014 was indeed a shop window for Golden Age TV.

During 2015, I was involved in a variety of productions that included *Father Brown*, *Call the Midwife* and *The Making of Dad's Army*, (We're Doomed!) which we filmed in and around the interesting city of Belfast. The part of Arthur Lowe as Captain Mainwaring was played to a T by the late John Sessions. John even had his head shaved to replicate Arthur Lowe's baldness. The set of the platoon's 'Church Hall' scene was replicated in a small community theatre on the outskirts of Belfast. All a long way from Television Centre and Thetford where the original series was filmed.

Also there was a five-part ITV drama series entitled *SS-GB* based on the 'what if the Nazis had won the war' novel by Len Deighton. Filming of one sequence, a joint Nazi/Soviet ceremony, took place at Highgate Cemetery. The Call Sheet for the day advised all to '*be aware of the sensitive nature of the programme and the possible upset that could be caused to the general public. Ensure that no costume or insignia are visible to the general public when leaving the set...*' in other words, no goose stepping around Golders Green in the lunch break, thank you very much! When transmitted, the news film cameras I had supplied were not seen at all, having hit the proverbial cutting room floor. Nothing new there.

Golden Age TV also filmed at Ely Cathedral in Cambridgeshire. This was part of our ongoing commission to provide camera props for the mammoth drama series produced by Netflix entitled *The Crown,* a very much expanded version of Peter Morgan's theatre production *The Audience.* This multi-part epic purports to follow the life and times of Her Majesty of recent memory. We helped recreate not only the BBC television 1953 coronation broadcast but also the newsreel sequence of Princess Elizabeth's wedding in 1947. On both occasions, Ely Cathedral stood in for Westminster Abbey. This might seem a bit perverse. So why not use the real building? But general practicalities always preclude this, especially in the heart of London. Usually, if a central London location is needed, the best time to film is early Sunday morning, mid-summer.

'The Crown' outside Ely Cathedral. Golden Age Tv vintage movie camera for 1947

But Ely Cathedral was fine and looked the part, even if the frigid wind whipping around the cloisters appeared to come direct from the Urals.

Another instructive experience was working again on a Hollywood movie. This was *The Infiltrator*, which starred *Breaking Bad* actor Bryan Cranston. *The Infiltrator is* a dramatic recreation of money laundering, drugs and the 1980s BCCI financial scandal. Our scenes, posing as NBCTV News cameramen, (this time wearing dinner jackets with black ties), were set during an elaborate wedding reception in a Florida ballroom circa July 1988. But in reality, filmed in March 2015 at a chilly hotel complex in Copthorne, West Sussex. That day we really felt for the unfortunate lady extras in their skimpy frilly Florida finery, as they stood in line outside, shivering and awaiting their cue to appear on set.

My part in *The Infiltrator* required me to actually film for real. I had supplied a 1980s vintage Sony Betacam BVP3 (anorak info) video camera and I was required to record a wedding sequence, the taped images to be intercut later within the main footage. During the wedding reception scene the FBI suddenly appears and breaks up the proceedings, charging in with guns and dogs. Lots of noise and racing about. Very dynamic. They hadn't told me that I was going to be part of the 'very dynamic' bit. The scene required that I was to be physically restrained from filming. So, I got a hefty whack from a charging extra, which bruised my eye and dislodged my finger from the camera's record button. The director loved it. Well that's alright then. Nurse, the screens!

Now, these early professional camcorders were not exactly lightweight objects. My task here was to wander around the set with one balanced on my shoulder. But the weight of this camera, and the long hours standing about, prompted me to pad my shoulder (under my jacket) with a quantity of bubble wrap. Unfortunately, every time I hoisted the camera onto my shoulder, ready to shoot, a loud 'popping' resulted, sounding like muffled gun shots. Bryan Cranston, awaiting his cue, remarked that my joints must be wearing out. I earned my money that day.

It's now time to jump back some biographical years to 1963. It's 2013 and the 50th anniversary of the *Doctor Who* programme. BBC2 had commissioned a celebratory drama and the producers sensibly came to the only guys on the planet capable of (again) recreating Lime Grove Studios, namely, Paul and me. This time the old BBC LG studio D (demolished in 1991) was constructed at the salubrious Wimbledon Studios, West London and for two weeks we all wallowed in TV nostalgia. Ace writer Mark Gatiss had lovingly crafted a script that beautifully recaptured the genesis of the programme. The story featured an eerily exact recreation of the original pilot episode studio recording. Character actor David Bradley played with exactitude William Hartnell playing Doctor Who. Other cast members included Claudia Grant as Susan, Jamie Glover as Chesterton and Jemma Powell as a spot-on Barbara. Paul and I installed our cameras, lights and gallery monitors and yes, yet again, undertook our timeless roles as television cameramen, wearing itchy beige pullovers and oily minimalist haircuts.

Some of the cast of 'An Adventure in Space
and Time'. Jessica Raine, David Bradley
Sacha Dhawan, Jamie Glover and
Jemma Powell

The opening of Dr Who. Seen in colour.

The Tardis and the last straw.

Studio clutter. Marco Polo

An Adventure in Space and Time began filming in February of 2013 with the 1963-era Lime Grove studio recreations taking about two weeks to complete. Our cameras again, were 'pretend live', in fact the same equipment as used on *The Hour*. Picky purists may have said that our cameras were not the *exact* models used in Studio D on the first *Doctor Who* programmes. We countered that our cameras were certainly used next door in Studio E, and in any case, none of the original *Doctor Who* Studio D cameras now exist (if at all) for prop hire purposes.

Our three Marconi cameras all had viewfinders that functioned and the red lights that glowed nicely when switched on. The camera's images were fed from the studio floor, directly to the gallery monitors. It all looked pretty authentic. Those pesky picky purists could probably tell that our 'old format' black and white images were somewhat too clean and sharp to pass for the real 1963 thing. The BBC sell-through DVD of the programme maintained the fiction that our cameras images were real. Not so. Bit naughty there. However, nothing broke down, everything ran all day and importantly, on cue. A little later, the director Terry McDonough created a break down all on his own.

Terry is a lovely chap and a skilled director but he was not so good with his hands. During a scene change, Terry decided to assist the props department and attempted to move one of our vintage 1960s trolleys with a monitor perched on top. Unfortunately, at that moment one of the trollies wheels came off and our precious original period monitor crashed to the floor. Fortunately there was no damage, apart from a small dent. They built 'em tough in those days. Not so amusing was later, when I very nearly put actor Brian Cox, playing Sydney Newman, in hospital. I was manoeuvring one of our heavy pedestals in preparation for a sequence and in an absent moment, bumped Brian in the back of his knees and the poor chap teetered, alarmingly. Fortunately, Brian regained his balance as I sheepishly reversed the ped in the nick of space and time.

I mentioned earlier I had had the pleasure of speaking with Carole Ann Ford. Other well-known actors wandered into the studio from time to time including Tom Goodman-Hill, (who played Mr Grove in ITV's drama series *Mr Selfridge*.) I'd met Tom previously when he had played a fleeting role as David Frost in a movie, filmed during 2007 called *Hippy Hippy Shake*. This controversial film, starring amongst others, Cillian Murphy, Sienna Miller, Chris O'Dowd, Lee Ingelby and Hugh Bonneville, purported to depict the UK's 1970s 'alternative culture'. The plot revolved around the concurrent underground press with the trial of the notorious *OZ* magazine 'School Kids Issue' featuring prominently.

Golden Age TV supplied various camera props including parking one of our large outside broadcast vehicles (Southern Television) on a private airfield in Buckinghamshire for a 'TV outside broadcast' scene. Our van was hired to help recreate the shambolic 1970 Isle of Wight pop festival. Sex, drugs and rock and roll? You bet! For this section of the movie, the airfield was bedecked with a large collection of prop 'merchandise' stalls, performance areas and lighting towers, plus an army of extras dressed as happy hippies. *Too* happy hippy as it turned out. Apart from the second camera unit filming a naked couple 'balling' (authentic 1970s term) behind our OB truck, what was most prevalent was the sweet smell of weed drifting all around. This was rather too much for the local Bucks constabulary, who arrived at reckless speed in true motorized *Sweeney* fashion to put a stop to all the fun. Sadly, despite the artistic effort and expense (north of £20 million), *Hippy Hippy Shake* sank with all on board. This movie, which had one or two preview showings, was never released theatrically or even dumped onto DVD. Finally, the unhappy hippy movie was shelved to fester somewhere in a dark Hollywood backroom. If reports are given credence, the entire negative has subsequently and irrevocably been shredded.

Returning to the impressive set of *An Adventure in Space and Time*, the specially constructed (and very expensive) Daleks used in the production were superb in every detail. I can attest to his having actually ridden in one of the originals. This occurred during the 1960s when I worked at Alexandra Palace, lending a hand with the annual BBC staff kids' Christmas party. As a timely surprise, we shipped from TV Centre your actual Dalek and I just had to have a ride, didn't I? My gosh, what an intractable object it was. All creaky wood and tatty bent tin. Not at all easy to shift, crouched inside, as one was, perched on a narrow bench, castors at each corner, trying to push along the bloody thing!

During a break in filming *An Adventure...* I spotted Peter Capaldi wandering around the set admiring the wonderfully recreated, TARDIS control console. I introduced myself and reminded him that we had worked together on Series Two of *The Hour* where Peter had played the part of Randell Brown. He remembered our association and I asked him whether he was a *Doctor Who* fan. He averred that he held a mild interest. '*I quite like the programme, Dicky...*' Later it was announced to all the world that he would be the next Doctor, so I suppose he really did 'quite like' the programme? The filming of *An Adventure in Space and Time* was a delight, a real highlight. As a lasting memento, I have a cast-signed shooting script.

Inside the Inside of Number 9

In 2016 Golden Age TV was commissioned to provide old style colour cameras for an episode of the comedy drama series *Inside Number. 9.* written and performed by Steve Pemberton and Reece Shearsmith. This exquisite show had been running on BBC2 to much acclaim, with each half hour episode featuring a location with a 'Number 9' in the mix. This time our cameras were going to shoot an *entire* episode, as the idea was to recreate a 1970s *Tales Of The Unexpected* type production, square screen, analogue tube fizz, glaring colour etc. Originally entitled 'Krampus', eventually, the episode was called *The Devil Of Christmas.*

Director Graeme Harper gives the cast last minute encouragement

The cast included Pemberton and Shearsmith, with Jessica Raine and Rula Lenska plus veteran tv director Graeme Harper calling the shots. The studio setting was a sort of Alpine lodge holiday cottage. Come the set-up day we carted four of our large studio cameras down to the BBC's Elstree Studio site at Borehamwood (actually Elstree is not particularly near Borehamwood but I would imagine that when filming began there in the 1920s and 1930s, the producers wanted to avoid critical comments such as 'another tedious production from **Boreham**wood!)

We installed our cameras in Studio D and tested the circuits to iron out any glitches, but nothing was amiss and we were ready to go. The idea was for director Graeme to cut from camera to camera in the production gallery, as was the practice back in the day. No problem. Indeed nothing went wrong.

Later when this episode was shown as a pre-view to a packed National Film Theatre audience-I sat next to Rula Lenska-the programme's producer indicated during an on-stage discussion that one of our cameras was, towards the end of the filming 'on the blink'. Complete fiction. Thanks very much Mr Producer.

We shot the entire *Inside No.9.* half hour episode in a day, with all the built-in scripted 'faults', mic shadows, camera lens hood in vision with creaky stilted acting (but not too much) and a few 'mistakes'. One scene called for the cast to carry suspiciously light 'holiday' suitcases, the reference being that in 'pretend' tv drama, suitcases don't need to be filled. A few years ago an actor who worked on the live Z-Cars 1960s production, told me that in rehearsals another cast actor had to carry the (empty) suitcase off 'on holiday' but come the live broadcast, the suitcase had, by cast members, been completely filled with several extremely heavy lead weights.

The Devil Of Christmas was well received, complete with it's 'surprise' ending, so I won't give it away here. Before it was transmitted, the producers had to get permission from the BBC to show it in a correct 4:3 aspect ratio. If I say so myself, whatever size they were, the pictures looked absolutely beautiful.

Hollywood Daze

It's 2017 and I'm off to LA to meet Laurel and Hardy. Well, no not really. Instead I meet Steve Coogan and John C. Reilly. It's at Twickenham Studios, West London. I'm there to add value to a new biopic movie currently being filmed recalling, in 1953, the time Laurel and Hardy toured the variety halls of Great Britain. The movie is *Stan and Ollie* and it premiered in 2018. It was well received and was a popular cinema hit of the year. (It's since been shown on BBC tv several times.)

Director Jon S. Baird and writer Jeff Pope had constructed a scene initially from Laurel and Hardy's 1937 movie *Way Out West.* Part of the scene was the dance routine sequence located outside Mickey Finn's bar. A mule tied to a hitching rail completed the ensemble. This was a really famous scene from *Way Out West* which we filmed all over again, so it had to be flawless.

Way Out West with my RKO 35mm movie camera

I had been hired to supply my 1930 Mitchell 35mm movie

camera (used originally by RKO at their Hollywood studios so absolutely genuine-in fact the only item on set that day that was.) Also, I was to play the part of 'cameraman'. The sequence involved back-chat between the principals and other dialogue. Me, I just fiddled away in the background, trying to look real. Dressed in authentic Californian sweater and sun cap, I positioned myself on a chair beside my camera and prepared to act on 'action'!

Steve Coogan and John C. Reilly re-created Stan and Ollie exactly. It was uncanny to watch them perform the well-rehearsed and familiar routines, take after take, considering also that John as Ollie was plastered in heavy prosthetics (completely undetectable close up) and costumed in a fitted 'fat suit' that needed regular gusts of cold air blasted up the trouser legs to keep John cool.

At the end of the shoot, a nice touch, John C. Reilly hired in an ice-cream van and gave the crew and cast free ice creams. If you have watched the movie, the opening sequence shows Stan and Ollie walk across a 'Hollywood' studio back-lot (filmed at Shepperton) and then walk through a studio door onto the set (at Twickenham). An instant cut of at least 25 miles between the locations. Ah, the magic of the movies.

My camera gets centre stage

Buckets of Blood and Lots of Gore

Gallows awaiting victims.

During the first half of 2019, Golden Age TV and me worked on a Warner Bros/DC tv production entitled *Pennyworth*. This drama series, set in an alternative 1960's British universe had as it's chief protagonist, an all-action ex-SAS hero called Alfred Pennyworth, who, in a later filmic incarnation became Batman's and Wayne Manor's very own live-in butler. Well, we all knew that didn't we?

For this series, the part of Alfred Pennyworth was played by a personable young actor named Jack Bannon, who had appeared previously in ITV's *Endeavour* as Sam, the son of DCI Fred Thursday. Jack Bannon approached the role of Pennyworth (or so it seemed to me) by re-imagining a 1960's version of the actor Michael Caine who, back in the day, had played Alfred Pennyworth in the original Batman series of movies. Now, not a lot of people know that.

One dark cold February morning, myself, colleague Paul, and patient wife Margaret arrived at the initial location, the old Royal Naval College at Greenwich. This location is often used for any scene depicting Georgian times, Victorian times, WW2 times and in this instance, hanging, draw and quartering times.

We duly installed some of our 1960's prop tv cameras in a courtyard, ready for the next days shooting schedule. The scene to be filmed was described on the call sheet as an 'execution of rebels' with several art department gallows awaiting the victims. Our cameras were an 'outside broadcast', there to transmit the scene live to an expectant home audience baying for blood, even if seen only in black and white. Around the gallows set was a seated audience of 150 people (the poor old 'extras' for this had to be on set at 4 o'clock in the morning!)

We assembled our vintage cameras on gantries, not any easy task as these veteran video machines are quite heavy and somewhat intractable. Whilst we laboured in the cause of cinematic art, others below us in the courtyard were practicing hanging themselves. Several stunt persons were rigging the various gibbets and dangling about on safety harnesses in order to get the right angles and to obtain verisimilitude. I mean, we didn't want it all to look ridiculous now did we?

Come the shoot day, the assembled extras filled the bleachers of the 'New Tyburn' set, the Arriflex cameras positioned themselves for their shots and the actors lined up to be choked and eviscerated on cue. Of course nobody was killed or even slightly scratched in the making of this movie. It just all looked like that.

When the director bawled 'action', the cameras zoomed in and framed up on an actor on the gallows. Then in came the props man with a bucket, the executioner then pretended to cut the actor in the belly. The props man then chucked a pail of 'giblets' towards the camera. Cut! (as it were). End of sequence. It all looked very authentic. Bit messy and it took a while clearing it all up afterwards, but director Danny Cannon and writer Bruno Heller were well pleased with the results. Took the best part of ten hours to obtain them. We all certainly needed guts on that day.

A few weeks later and we were all at Hatfield House outside in a back field with the same old-style tv cameras, this time filming a 'Raven Society' rally. A flag waving and stiff-arm saluting, dark shirts, Heil! That sort of rally. I met Anna Chancellor again, appearing here as part of the Pennyworth cast in a scene where she had to address 500 chanting-crowd extras. Also included in the shot were several thuggish baton-wielding (soft rubber) police extras and a dozen or so mounted horses, one of which had to ride straight up onto the rally stage. Quite spectacular, and bloody dangerous. Stunt men certainly cut it fine, but equally skilful and aware of all safety parameters. I did notice later that the 'armorer', the chap who looked after the firearms used in the scene had only one hand.

A later scene was less hazardous. Moving into a room at Hatfield House, here young actress Jessica Ellerby, (playing a version of the Queen), addressed the nation on tv. Pennyworth was standing by as a bodyguard. The scene rolled, the Queen at her desk spoke to a tv camera that I had provided and after the broadcast, as she left, as part of the scene she whispered something into Pennyworth's ear. I don't know what Jessica said in Jack Bannon's ear, but standing close by I could have sworn I saw young Jack blush!

Royal broadcast set

I Was Kylie's Cameraman

When I filmed Kylie Minogue for the first time, it went like this. Award-winning director Sophie Muller contacted me, asking if I would film a few scenes for Kylie Minogue's latest song 'Say Something', being shot that following week in a studio near Acton. The song would have a *1980s* 'disco' feel so they wanted some *Top Of The Pops* sparkle, wobble and smeary lights. Easy, as I had provided the same quality many times previously for other groups, many of whom have since completely and mysteriously faded from popular memory.

Come the shoot day, I arrived at the studio to find it strewn with sets, props and personnel filling every conceivable space. Not much room for me and my small 30 year-old Sony video camera. Sophie Muller explained that all the main action was being filmed *hi res* and my video shooting would be inserted into the finished product as 'contrast'. I was told to film a performance, grab shots and nip about as best I could to get different angles. This suited me as it gave me freedom to experiment, but I kept to the main commission which was to make it *Top Of The Pops*. So lots of pointing the camera directly into lights, defocussing the image and drifting off to the left or right, but strictly on the beat. This is important. Filming music has it's own rhythm.

Kylie changed costumes a lot during that day. At one point Kyle was dressed entirely in Bacofoil. Various scenes were shot with a big and complicated digital camera and I had to wait my turn. Eventually I was squeezed in front of a platform directly under a rather large and threatening camera crane. Kyle arrived in her final costume change and the big digi camera and my small analogue camera prepared, as instructed, to film from several different angles. Now, old style colour cameras need quite a bit of light, modern digital cameras hardly any. I was just about getting an image on my camera so I cranked up the 'gain' control which made the picture a bit 'noisy' but Sophie Muller thought it 'fantastic'. With that directorial endorsement I pressed 'record' and commenced to film the diminutive Aussie.

Time flies when you're having fun, and soon the filming finished and became a 'wrap'. All good with just a 20 minute break whilst the DIT (digital interface technician) down-loaded the memory stick (an old style analogue video signal has to be first converted before it can be recorded into digits).

A month or two later Kylie's *Say Something* music video hit the internet and what a lovely, sparkly, visual treat it was. But not one single frame of what I had shot that day appeared! Bit of a disappointment, but this happens. Sometimes I can provide a load of images, but not one of which will make the final cut.

Later browsing the internet, I noticed that Kylie Minogue was advertised as having appeared on NBC's *The Tonight Show* with Jimmy Fallon. A frame grab from her appearance looked familiar. I tuned in and watched agog as Kyle performed 'live' her *Say Something* song. This entire television performance was not the glossy hi res music video. It was instead, *everything* I had shot on my little Sony video camera, skilfully edited together and purporting to be Kylie 'live' in the New York studio. Which of course it wasn't. Subsequent internet chat comments: "Hey guys, how did you get that wonderful *retro* look?!" I *could* tell them a story......

Kylie sings for my camera and the USA audience

Video Daze

Incidentally, I once spent the night with Kylie. It's true. It happened at a bijou Soho restaurant and things got really hot around midnight! But I should be so lucky. Actually, I was there to film *The Kiss Of Life* her latest music video and we started to shoot at the witching hour. It was the only time we could film, after the restaurant had closed for the evening. So from 12 o'clock until 10am the following day we cranked our cameras whilst London slept on, oblivious. Us come the dawn, stumbling out, bleary eyed.

Pop promos or music videos as they are currently referred to are nothing if not colourful. I've filmed dozens. Who can now recall seeing anything I shot with Ordinary Boys, A1, Damage, Pink Grease, Estelle, British Whale, Late Of The Pier, Topper, Lowfinger, TSD, Wiley, Do Me Bad Things, Colour Of Fire, Ikara Colt, Donkey Boys, Ordinary Boys, Golden Silvers, Robert Post. Pato Banton, Dum Dums, Ali Love, New Young Pony Club, Lost Prophets, Moloko, Kinesis, The Kills, Baddies, Dead?

Perhaps we can all still remember The Horrors? Noisy lot. I filmed them three times at different locations and singing different 'songs'. One location was an old disused sewage pumping station near Erith in Kent. Atmospheric. On this occasion, I was given to use, a small 16mm camera loaded with a cassette of film. All went okay until the camera started to make a sort of grinding noise every time I tilted it. Also, I fell backwards at one point, nearly hitting my head on a metal beam. The director rushed over more concerned for the bloody camera, (which was on hire)

Eventually the completed video arrived and my 'grinding' pictures, (sort of slipping creating a jerky sliding image), were actually used. Apparently this happy happenstance was something that the director thought was 'cool' and the Horrors were pleased. Hooray!

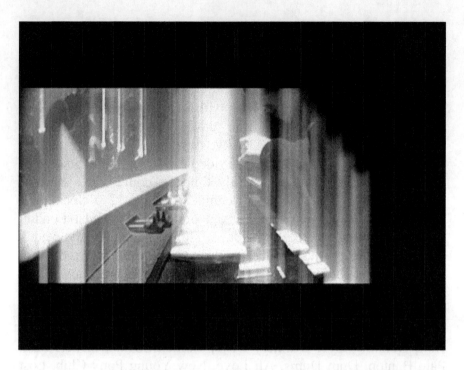

The result of my 'faulty' 16mm camera. Good effect though.

Another Horrors occasion was a club venue at The Elephant and Castle in London. This time it was more than a bit rackety as we had a boisterous audience to add 'colour'. Before we began to shoot I trained a spotlight on the lead singer who shrieked that it was too bright and could I turn it off! I explained that I needed the light to film by otherwise the Horrors would be in complete darkness. Not the idea at all really.

In August 2005 I filmed the Arctic Monkeys and their first number one single *I Bet You Look Good On The Dance Floor.* The director wanted a 1980s 'look' so I wheeled in two of my large and really very heavy 1980s studio cameras. The studio space we used was owned by MTV but was formerly the Camden HQ of TVAM, the original 'Roland Rat' breakfast tv station with the egg cups on the building's gables.

Usually, musicians and singers mime to a playback of a previously recorded song, but on this occasion the Arctic's recorded live the entire track in the studio and then mimed to that playback. It shows my ignorance, when earlier, wandering into the control room

118

I saw some lads fiddling with controls. I asked if they were the recording technicians. 'No, we're the band', came the pithy reply.

I filmed Ben Drew otherwise known as Plan B at the RAK Studio near Regents Park in West London. RAK is a famous place for musicians, founded in 1976 by record producer Mickie Most, who was known for his hits with The Animals, Jeff Beck, Donovan, Suzi Quatro and Kim Wilde, among others, but a bit cramped for filming. We began shooting and then I noticed on the monitors that our pictures were beginning to 'hum'. That's where a faint grey band moves slowing down the picture. What could we do? Actually nothing much. The whole place was an electronics box with amps and large speakers everywhere. We were being interfered with, electrically. The next time I filmed Ben, it was at a slightly larger venue, the O2 Arena! Plenty of space there.

Ben Drew and Plan B seen here through the mist of creativity at RAK Studios

Another filming venue was at Abbey Road and in the legendary 'Beatles' Studio Two. Singer Paolo Nutini wanted some of his tunes filmed using again Golden Age TV's old tube colour cameras. The tracks were *Iron Sky* and *Let Me Down Easy* from his 2014 album 'Caustic Love' Unfortunately for us, Paolo insisted on rehearsing with his band at top volume. I mean really *very* loud. Unnecessarily loud. Poor old me desperately trying to line up and coax our old cameras into some sort of life, ready for recording (colleague Paul was running the video recorders) whilst in the background our star performer belted out his songs at top db. Worth it in the end I suppose. Latest figures for on-line viewing of these Nutini songs are currently north of 75 million.

Abbey Road Studio 2 and Paolo Nutini warming up for the Golden Age TV classic cameras

Moving on, I had filmed The Coral previously in 2007 at Twickenham Studios Stage One. I recall it was something of a bad tempered shoot. Not least because it dragged on way past midnight and involved a large motion control rig which kept malfunctioning.

On that extended day I was using a Japanese Ikegami video camera which worked unflinchingly, as one might have reasonably expected from a top-of-the- range 1980s electronics product.

Several years later in 2019 and it's The Coral again. This time Liverpool and an abandoned warehouse, winter time and chilly. My rig this time was an ex-BBC Scotland portable camera which had the added bonus of a built-in star filter. This gives a nice sparkly effect on lights. Very useful as it definitely added value to the scenes photographed. A small Vinten pedestal completed the ensemble, although an old warehouse floor is not exactly studio quality smooth, so several tracking shots wobbled a bit.

Bags of fun with The Coral in Liverpool. Sweet Release

The Coral were perfect subjects this time. 'Sweet Release' was the song. Also, a local young dance group had been roped in to perform a routine wearing large brown paper bags over their heads. Several as it transpired because the 'smiley' faces on the bags changed to 'frowns' and 'grimaces' as the tune progressed, so the bags were swapped several times throughout the day. By 'wrap' time we all congratulated ourselves. Everything was safely in the can and definitely 'in the bag'.

Here are several more promo images and related musical stuff. All good fun to film. One promo track lasted *nine* minutes which took a bit of stamina on my part. The eye can get a bit bleary squinting down a viewfinder all day long. Doesn't do much for ones back bones either.

Martin Solveig, RAYE and Jax Jones. I filmed their song
Tequila LA LA LA. *A delight, especially Raye's costume!*
Catch the song on Vevo

Jax Jones and RAYE on camera

Not The King but a Horrible Histories *episode about Elvis on tv.
I supplied the genuine USA tv camera. The wretched HHTV sticker
absolutely ruined the paintwork when I tried to peel it off*

This appears to be a photo of the BBC's Old Grey Whistle Test? *No to that. It's Twickenham Studios, a few years ago and I filmed this set entirely on my own with a single video camera and a few lights. The song ran for nine minutes and it's called **Funny Farm**. The musicians are Dworniak Bone Lapsa, a session band.*

The final filmed result looks exactly *like a genuine BBC four-camera shoot at Television Centre Studio 8. As it was meant to....*

Late Of The Pier. 'Fokker' Minimal set all in green.

Mabes 'Caught Up' grabbed off the screen.

New Young Pony Club. Forgotten what that was about.

Ronika and chums. 'Marathon' This was filmed in a large garage.

Britain's Got No Talent. *That was me in 1958 attempting to sing at a Southend- on-Sea band stage competition. I didn't win a prize mainly due to my off-key rendition of 'I've Got A Lovely Bunch Of Coconuts' The audience laughed, so at least I got a reaction.*

The Last Shadow Puppets
Symphonic pop from Alex (Arctic Monkeys) Turner
Song 'Standing Next To Me'. I supplied the prop camera for this
promo which was filmed in one continuous take using a Steadicam.

Alex Turner again with the Arctic Monkeys. A set for the BBC at
Maida Vale Studios. Cameras from Golden Age TV

Pilot Lights

I've made quite a few pilots. That is to say, provisional programmes that either later get commissioned as a series or disappear into a video black hole never to shine by the light of the silvery phosphor again. The most recent request hired two of my 1940's BBC microphones. I wasn't told very much about the project, (as usual) only that it was a pilot for something or other, and that the microphones were to be used in an 'old' radio studio. Subsequent investigations revealed that the 'old radio studio' was actually a room in the Secret Nuclear Bunker at Kevedon Hatch near Brentwood in Essex. Well waddayaknow?

Another pilot programme involved some colourful Spanish practices. This was *La Princesa de Woking,* written and starring Emma Sidi, and aadapted from her 2016 critically acclaimed sell-out Edinburgh Fringe show 'Telenovela'. This short drama was filmed entirely in the Spanish language at a palatial villa in Barnet North London. Essentially, *La Princesa de Woking* is a comedy pastiche, a type of 1980s creaky wobbly *Crossroads* of Latin America, but played straight with over-emphasized acting styles and non-sequitur dialogue. It sounds excruciating and corny but it worked
beautifully.

The 'body' seems to be missing.

I provided two analogue portable colour cameras which provided an image that replicated a cathode ray tube quality of the period. The interior of the house was 'set decorated' with additional props, pictures, table lamps and a coffin on a bier. Yes, all part of the action. Even a body in the coffin. One sequence required an actress to fall down a flight of stairs. For this, a stunt man was used. He was dressed in the same clothes plus wig and on 'action' tumbled nicely downwards. The stunt man had a beard, but this was all part of the scene. A very brief cut from actress to stunt man and back again with actress on the floor at the foot of the stairs. The eagle-eyed might have spotted the beard on the way down....

The large house we were filming in had been hired for the day. (on a previous shoot at a domestic location I had asked what sort of damage insurance was needed. £10 million quid mate, said the director. So that was a comfort).

At lunch time, the *de Woking* cast and crew decamped to a local pub. Food was provided along with a glass of lager. Very nice but quite unusual this. Normally, during working hours, alcohol (and smoking) are banned from studios. Makes sense, of course, but in sunny Barnet, on that day we all appreciated a swift half and were back in time for part two, all steady of hand and clear of gimlet eye.

131

You may now ask, what became of the pilot of *La Princesa de Woking*? It had its chance to be commissioned as a tv comedy series, but unfortunately, it never was. However, it did get seen. It was screened on the festival circuit, having played at the Chicago Comedy Film festival, New Orleans Comedy Film Festival, London Comedy Film Festival and the Canadian International Comedy Film Festival. Latterly, BBC 2 aired it (at 11.30pm on a Tuesday) so a couple of other people saw it too. The drama lasted for ten minutes and after it had finished I watched the end credits rolling and there was my name as cameraman. Very nice. I had to translate it though, it was all in Spanish.

Setting the camera kit through the Barnet mansion door. When the movie scene cut to the 'supposed' exterior, it showed a tiny bungalow.

Back to the Grind

So what ever happened to my rock-solid determination never ever in a million years, cross my heart and hope to die, to draw another cartoon? It was that devil Tim Quinn of course. He contacted me about a publication he was editing for the charity, Liverpool Heartbeat. Tim was assembling a magazine that was going to describe the history of various statues in and around the city of Liverpool. Apparently the area is littered with them. Sounded extremely interesting, I must say. Tim asked me if I could think of something funny to fill a page. Also, he offered me money, which concentrated my mind somewhat.

What a wonderful resource the internet is. In a very few hours I had trawled it, looking for illustrations and photographs of Liverpool monuments and various erections of the great and good. My *Statue Of Limitations* cartoon page was the result, which may have raised a chuckle or two? But then Tim was at it again. 'What about some more Dr Who stuff, (see our latest book *Who's 60-A Celebration of Whos?*) more Marvel stuff, (see our latest book- *The Fantastic 400- The Worlds Largest Superhero Team*), autobiographies, (see etc...) personal appearances on the media, comic conventions... hang about Tim, aren't we in danger here of going all the way back to **Page One**?

"He's a very slow reader!"

Tail Pieces

A selection of cartoons and images plus bits I forgot to add earlier.

My very latest Dr Who cartoon page featuring the new Doctor in 'Who's 60? A Celebration of Whos' a recent New Haven book by Tim Quinn and myself.

Some of my personal favourite **Whos** and others...

A DAY IN THE LIFE OF A DOCTOR WHO SET DESIGNER

139

THE EXCLUSIVE DOCTOR WHO CLUB

You've been bouncing him on your knee again haven't you.....

I reckon Batman's over the limit..

Extract from a series in a model railway magazine

Hulk The Menace, being a Hooligan as usual

143

All Get Set

Taking snaps on set is generally not allowed. I get away with it by claiming it's for 'insurance purposes'. Here are a few examples that I managed to snatch during rehearsals.

Tom Baker arguing with the director. We filmed him for a SHADA 'lost episode' sell–through BBC DVD. SHADA written by Douglas Adams was mostly recorded in 1979 but abandoned due to industrial action. BBC World reconstituted and edited the stored video tape footage with additional scenes filmed by myself to match the original image quality.

Yes it's Jamie Oliver looking a right prawn.
Some sort of Ch4 programme promotion.

Spot the dummy! Cost saving exercise. Crowd
scenes dressed to please. No complaints heard,
toilet breaks or meals taken. We all look stoned..

*2012. Filming a tv drama 'Bert and Dickie' by
the Thames near Windsor. Matt Smith (then a Dr
Who) caught me photographing him. I pretended to take a snap of
my tv camera prop.*

*Sheridan Smith as CILLA in a recent ITV Cilla
Black biopic. During a scene Sheridan sang
unaccompanied live. The music backing was dubbed
on later. Talented lady.*

Jason Isaacs as Harry H Corbett as Harold Steptoe

We don't often get the chance to stick our hand up the bottom of a celebrity! This is dear old SOOTY who visited my garage to be filmed for a short documentary. This particular puppet was used for stage appearances, so is larger that the original.

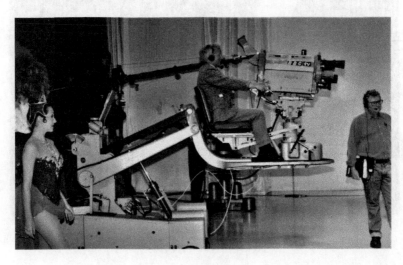

Crane driver and showgirl. What fun we had!

A scene for an episode of George Gently, filmed in Newcastle. On this occasion, we rigged our cameras to give a picture on the viewfinder, Normally our props are what's known as 'Non Prac'. To give a 'live' look we implant small modern electronics. Original working condition (if it could be achieved) would be cost-prohibitive and a bit pointless anyway.

Goodwood Revival. *2022. Classic cameras with audience participation. Firm favourite at the event.*

'1970s' Press Conference. A camera displays an image on the monitor.
Drama series 'Whitehouse Farm' The live Ikegami 79D news camera is over 40 years old. It always amazes me that these cameras are still producing reasonable images. Mind you, all the electronic components are gold tipped, and the camera was made in Japan.....

Filming a pantomime horse for a village panto.
The local racecourse steward, who hadn't been
forewarned (we had asked permission) came
rushing over. He thought we were climate
protesters!

Hippy No Great Shakes

The shredded movie HIPPY HIPPY SHAKE *scenes*
outside the Old Bailey and Courts of Appeal.

Impressionist Jon Culshaw, recreating Patrick Moore for a Sky At Night *Special*

The real two

The set of the Church Hall for 'We're Doomed
The Making Of Dad's Army' *The location was a small arts
theatre studio near Belfast*

*John Sessions as Captain Mainwaring and Julian Sands as Sgt
Wilson. Both superb depictions. My cameras had 'pretend' working
with a picture on a monitor to add realism to the scene. Both
camera types would have been used at the BBC Television Centre
Studio 4 in 1968*

We get on local tv (again). My daughter Lucy and me at the Anglia Tv studios in Norwich. A 1988 Telethon. (Biddings are closed now). Hulk The Menace peeking through.

A production Thank You *card from* Call The Midwife. *Nice to be appreciated. Nice people too.*

The Infiltrator *movie 'wedding reception' scene. Golden Age colleagues Richard and Paul line up one of our cameras. The location ; a disused hotel near Gatwick airport.*

All mod cons. Our technical base for this movie was a ladies toilet.

USA embassy? Nope. Walthamstow Town Hall. Me and my camera for a Mercedes commercial. December. They had to clear the snow away as it was supposed to be July.

A still from a Horrors video. Breath taking quality

History it Isn't

Looks like Chamberlain with his little piece of paper at Heston aerodrome in 1938? Nein. All cameras and mics supplied by Golden Age Tv. A scene from the reboot series of Upstairs Downstairs *of a few years ago. Took all day to set up. Plane flew in, actors lined up. Cameras whirred. Scene never used.*

Churchill's funeral? 1965. Nope. A scene from
The Crown *(never used)*

Me and my Bolex H16 movie camera in 1967. Mod haircut, when I had hair to cut...

Sad state of the old BBC studios at Alexandra Palace in the 1990s. Bit better now perhaps?

Scrap yard where I found eight old tv cameras. Quite a bit of restoration required.

MUNICH. *A few tons of tv equipment in a hanger awaiting the choice of Mr Spielberg*

Cartoon Capers

Marvel Comic. **Forces In Combat**

Acne *comic. My take on God.*

Drew this series for a Norwich-based magazine
Never got paid.

ACNE *comic. Play on words*

'SMUT' Tasteless 'alternative' humour. Best forgotten

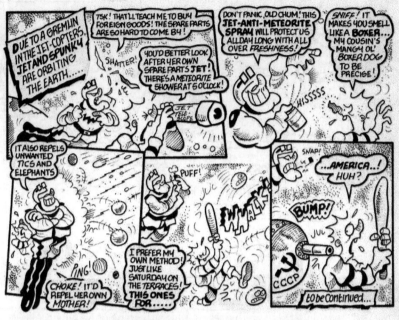

The BBC World Wide Boy. Ariel magazine article. Management not best pleased with my 'humour'.

Great Britain themed postcard. Bit rude perhaps for the tourist trade?

Trial cartoon strips. Jury's still out.

Cloth-ears, I said can you play 'In The Mood'...!

All set ready to film, complete with 1980s costume and ginger wig. The things we do for money.

Lots of film cameras, mics and lights for an exhibition at Duxford, (part of the Imperial War Museum). It was a cinema-themed weekend in 2019. Some scenes for the 1969 movie The Battle Of Britain *were filmed at Duxford. Home also during WWII of the US Eighth Airforce 78th fighter group.*

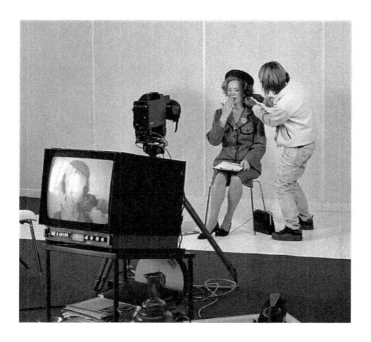

Leslie Duncan as Margaret Thatcher. Tiring day?

Another scene from The Hour. *Joshua McGuire on the 16mm camera. Ben Whishaw to the right and in the centre, the future* Comoran Strike *actor Tom Burke.*

Margaret guarding the cameras, her usual task.

A video grab of Quinn and Howett flogging a comic.
Anglia Tv with presenter Graham Bell. Nice little cut out figures on
the desk, something 3D for the cameras to focus on

Acne Comic or was it Smut Comic?

*Thus was a cover illustration for a proposed memoire of Dr Who
producer John Nathan Turner. It was to reprint Dr Who
programme 'diary' extracts published previously by Nathan Turner
in Dr Who Magazine. Nothing ever came of this project, but I was
quite pleased with my drawing, especially the Tardis pencil case.*

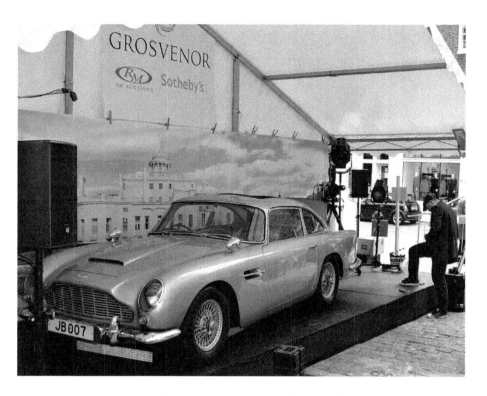

An original James Bond Aston Martin DB5.
This was up for auction and I was asked to
provide film equipment, camera and lights,
(seen at the back) to 'dress' the scene. The
alfresco location was New Bond Street in
London and later, invited guests gathered to
admire the setting. I think the auction reserve
price was in the low millions. All were shaken
but not stirred.

Oh, didn't I mention the Family Curse....?

Golden Age Tv displays, at the opening of the BBC's New Broadcasting House, one of the tv cameras discovered in a Chelmsford junk yard. Hours of restoration required, but the camera now looks brand new. In fact probably better than it did when the BBC first used it in 1953.

Fear Of Fanny. *A 2011 BBC4 biopic of cooking guru Fanny Cradock. Just seen in this studio shot, (taken at the since demolished Teddington Studios), is Mark Gatiss as Johnnie and Julia Davis as Fanny.*

Kylie green screens for Dicky's camera.

The Best Possible Taste. *A 2012 BBC4 drama about the life and times of Kenny Everett. Seen here in front of me and my EMI 2001 camera is actor Oliver Lansley who recreated Kenny magnificently. Pitch-perfect, the producers had despaired originally of finding a suitable player for the role, until they found Oliver. The image on the monitor is via a small modern CCD camera placed at the front under the large camera's lens to give the effect of a live image. The scene was supposed to be the studio of ITV company Thames. (actually Studio 2 BBC Television Centre) There is no 'Thames' badge as would have been usual on the camera. The copyright holders of the Thames name were asking too large a usage fee. C'est la Vie.*

FAMOUS DALEKS

JOHN LOGIE DALEK
INVENTOR OF
TELEVISION

A page from Who's 60? A Celebration of WHOS. *New Haven Publishing have produced this new anniversary edition. It's a selection from some of our Dr Who Magazine cartoons and books with new material. However, Sylvester McCoy doesn't look too happy about it for some reason.*

A Marvel Comics series The Concise
History Of The Galaxy. *Note the
talking toilet bowl. Mr Quinn at his best.*

*I never did get to draw Jodie W in a magazine. This was a
complimentary card. Looks almost like her too..*

*Trevor Eve as Hughie Green in another BBC tv
biopic,* Most Sincerely. *I noticed that Trevor studied his lines by
staring at a page of the open script on the floor in front of him. A
consummate actor, it would seem that this was the way he
approached the learning of lines. Always a mystery to me.*

It was originally an 'ayatollah' doll..oops..

Kerry Katona in Showbands. *A 2005 TV movie featuring a particular aspect of 1960's Irish popular musical entertainment. Golden Age TV provided studio cameras for two series of* Showbands *filmed in County Galway. The drama was aired mainly in the republic of Ireland via RTE (Radio Teilifis Eireann)*

Emoting musically.

The Wimbledon Theatre, a scene where we supplied 'working' cameras for the 2014 Tommy Cooper drama Not Like This- Like That. *David Threlfall played a magical re-enactment of Tommy. The scene here was re-creating Tommy's death on stage during a live ITV variety show in 1984.*

185

Watch the birdie. Feathered visitor perched on our camera.
Showbands *studio.*

A pre- CD cartoon. I suppose CDs melt too?

Filming during Covid precautions. That's why we are wearing masks, not because of the SFX mist. I'm manning my American 1950's RCA camera (very rare) for a National Geographic Channel documentary about boxer Muhammad Ali

My precious things...

Printed by BoD™in Norderstedt, Germany